UNIVERSITY COLLEGE

BERYL IVEY LIBRARY

DATA LOVE

THE SEDUCTION AND BETRAYAL
OF DIGITAL TECHNOLOGIES

ROBERTO SIMANOWSKI

Columbia University Press *New York*

Columbia University Press
Publishers Since 1893
New York   Chichester, West Sussex
cup.columbia.edu
Copyright © Matthes & Seitz Berlin Verlagsgesellschaft mbH 2014.
All rights reserved by and controlled through Matthes & Seitz Berlin Verlag
English translation © 2016 Columbia University Press
Translated from the German by Brigitte Pichon and Dorian Rudnytsky,
with the assistance of John Cayley, Luciana Gattass, and the author.

Library of Congress Cataloging-in-Publication Data
Names: Simanowski, Roberto, author.
Title: Data love : the seduction and betrayal of digital technologies /
Roberto Simanowski.
Other titles: Data love. English
Description: New York : Columbia University Press, [2016] | Translation
from German. | Includes bibliographical references and index.
Identifiers: LCCN 2016002787 (print) | LCCN 2016013214 (ebook) |
ISBN 9780231177269 (cloth : alk. paper) | ISBN 9780231542425 (e-book) |
ISBN 9780231542425 ()
Subjects: LCSH: Internet—Social aspects. | Internet—Moral and ethical aspects. |
Digital communications—Social aspects. | Privacy, Right of.
Classification: LCC HM851 .S554713 2016 (print) | LCC HM851 (e-book) |
DDC 302.23/1—dc23
LC record available at http://lccn.loc.gov/2016002787

Columbia University Press books are printed on permanent and
durable acid-free paper.
This book is printed on paper with recycled content.
Printed in the United States of America

c 10 9 8 7 6 5 4 3 2 1

COVER DESIGN: Philip Pascuzzo

For Luciana
Whom I love more than any data

Lots of knowledge fits into a hollow head.

—Karl Kraus, *Dicta and Contradicta* (1909)

And youth is cruel, and has no remorse
And smiles at situations which it cannot see.

—T. S. Eliot, "Portrait of a Lady" (1920)

He was found by the Bureau of Statistics to be
One against whom there was no official complaint,
And all the reports on his conduct agree
That, in the modern sense of an old-fashioned word, he was a saint.

—W. H. Auden, "The Unknown Citizen" (1939)

CONTENTS

Preface xi

PART I: BEYOND THE NSA DEBATE

1 Intelligence Agency Logic 3

2 Double Indifference 8

3 Self-Tracking and Smart Things 13

4 Ecological Data Disaster 17

5 Cold Civil War 24

PART II: PARADIGM CHANGE

6 Data-Mining Business 35

7 Social Engineers Without a Cause 39

8 Silent Revolution 44

9 Algorithms 50

10 Absence of Theory 59

PART III: THE JOY OF NUMBERS

11 Compulsive Measuring 67

12 The Phenomenology of the Numerable 72

13 Digital Humanities 80

14 Lessing's Rejoinder 87

PART IV: RESISTANCES

15 God's Eye 97

16 Data Hacks 102

17 On the Right Life in the Wrong One 113

Epilogue 119

Postface 122

Notes 129

Index 151

PREFACE

PRAISED be the technology that allows us to listen to Berlin's "Info Radio" in the Swiss Alps or in a Hong Kong subway! Praised be the city map that describes itself when clicked on and—without our having to study it—leads us to the place we seek! Praise also to Shazam and all the apps that identify an unknown song, directly linking us to both the lyrics and the video! Praise to the online travel plan, showing all our connections within seconds and selling us the ticket as well! And likewise praised be the asthma inhaler that uses GPS to warn other patient-users away from those areas that they should avoid!

We love information. We always have. We used to gather around early wanderers to hear tales of faraway places when it was rare to find books outside of monasteries. We invented the telegraph because we grew impatient waiting for travelers. We waited as eagerly for the morning paper as for the evening news on radio or on TV, as if they were only ever presenting good news. Now we get the latest news by the minute, and we even treat our own lives as news, updating ourselves around the clock via Facebook, Twitter, or Instagram. Our eagerness to share information matches our greed for taking it in.

We view every mountain and every lake that has not yet been surveyed as an insult to human reason. When we communicate, watch videos, jog, eat, or sleep, a limitless fervor drives us to access the networks of ourselves and our social life. We are on a mission to produce data ceaselessly and in perpetuity. Every tweet is regarded as a contribution to knowledge. We believe in progress through analysis, which will make our lives easier and more secure.

We love ourselves in the form of the blue arrow on Google's map, and we eagerly anticipate the advent of the smart city where all citizens' movements are tracked, creating instant taxi stands wherever they happen to be needed. We're looking forward to the "wearable computers" that will permit us to remain online without taking our hands off the steering wheel. We thank Google for reminding us where we are, what we should know, and what we will want to do next.

An information society is one in which all information is just seconds away, information about everything, everywhere, and at all times: "information at your fingertips." We live in an information society. And we love it!

In 2011 the title of a Berlin conference called Data Love was justified in the following way:

> Today, data is what electricity has been for the industrial age. Business developers, marketing experts and agency managers are faced with the challenge to create new applications out of the ever-growing data stream with added value for the consumer. In our data-driven economy, the consumer is in the focus point of consideration. Because his behaviour determines who wins, what lasts and what will be sold. Data is the crucial driver to develop relevant products and services for the consumer.[1]

This emphatic promotion is affirmed by the classic business adage: "What can't be measured can't be managed." Both statements show that data love is in no way unconditional. It is devoted to data as information that gives a meaningful form to measurable facts.[2]

To be sure, "data love" is a euphemism. It is the palatable alternative to the central concept of digital-information society: big-data mining—the computerized analysis of large collections of data intended to reveal regularities and previously unknown correlations. "Love" refers to both aspects of the dual nature of the mining: Corporations love big data because it allows them to develop customized products, and consumers love big data for the same reason. This, at least, is what the quotation proposes to us: Mining data leads to added value for customers. Data love is a phenomenon not only of the society of control but also of the consumer society. And data love thrives on precisely the same data that security and privacy would claim to protect.

At the same time, data love is embraced by Internet activists who advocate free communication and proclaim as "principles of datalove" that data must flow, must be used, is neither good nor bad nor illegal, cannot be owned, is free. This notion opposes "the misconceptions of politicians, who keep trying to establish exceptions for the expression of certain types of data"—such as "hate speech" or "child porn"—and postulates an unconditional love of data regardless of that data's nature or possible misuse: "Datalove is so exciting! It's all about the availability of data. What people do with it is not the question. The point is: people need data. Need to get it. Need to give it. Need to share it. Need to do things with it, by means of it." This is another and different form of data love, conceptualized as a desire to know or even as a second wave of Enlightenment: "Datalove is about appreciation of being able to understand, perceive and process data altogether for the enjoyment and progress of all sentient beings." Business entrepreneurs and marketing experts can easily subscribe to this call for free data flow. What is missing in this enthusiastic embrace of data is a sensitivity to the potential for conflict between data mining and privacy. Claiming that "if some data is meant to be private, it should not reach the Internet in the first place" sounds an awful lot like the rhetorically effective "nothing-to-hide" argument one generally hears from intelligence agencies and big software companies.[3]

This book describes the promises and dangers of data's ambivalent love. It discusses the changes affecting the human situation and considers data love not as the obsessive behavior of overzealous intelligence agencies, clever businessmen, and Internet (h)ac(k)tivists but rather as the entanglement of all those who—whether out of stinginess, convenience, ignorance, narcissism, or passion—contribute to the amassing of ever-more data about their lives, eventually leading to the statistical evaluation and profiling of their individual selves.

Those who discuss the NSA scandal of the summer of 2013 only as a matter of the tension between the two basic rights to freedom and security are failing to see the more problematic or even aporetic aspect of the issue. The imperative of transparency implemented by social online portals, self-tracking applications, and the promises of the Internet renders data gathering an everyday phenomenon. What is technologically feasible becomes all but universally irresistible. Naturally, this is especially true when it comes to intelligence agencies. But the same circumstances hold for the consumer economy and for those in charge of infrastructural government, that is, traffic control, urban planning, public-health administration, etc. The majority of people are looking forward to all the promises of data mining. Herein lies the philosophical problem that goes beyond the political discussion of the NSA scandal. Data love leads to a double-edged potentiality: the reconciliation of society with its security apparatus. In the age of increasing digitization of human communication, the logical consequence for everyone is the so-called full take of all data on everyone and everything. Against our wishes and our declarations to the contrary, privacy in the twenty-first century becomes outdated.

The effects of this unrestrained exploitation of personal data have been compared with ecological disaster. It is maintained that just as the individual use of energy is not a merely personal matter, so dealing with personal data has social consequences with ethical implications. A discussion from this perspective goes beyond the easy citizen-versus-state logic. However, simultaneously, it undermines our thinking through the problem in a new way. For while the ecological movement's ethics are focused on the preservation of human existence—which no one would oppose—the concept of "data disaster" basically operates in relation to a culturally conservative position for which privacy is a value that should remain untouched. This idea of privacy as an inalienable right is compromised by the willingness—not only of the younger generation—to give up personal data and, inadvertently, by all those who blindly agree to insidious terms of service. If, in the context of the NSA scandal, people have talked about a "cold civil war," then this should be understood as a conflict *within* every citizen—namely, between an interest in data mining's advantages and a fear of its disadvantages.

The principal agencies of big-data mining are the number crunchers and the data scientists whose current job descriptions increase in sex appeal and promise remuneration in the millions. Unnoticed and inexorably, their contributions to increasingly efficient methods of data management and analysis are changing cultural values and social norms. Software developers are the new utopians, and their only program for the world is programmability, occasionally garnished with vague expressions of the emancipatory value of participation and transparency. The secret heroes of this "silent revolution" are the algorithms that are taking over humanity. On the one hand, they increasingly assume "if-then" directives, enforcing them immediately and relentlessly. On the other hand, they reveal more and more if-then correlations and, armed with this new knowledge, pressure society to intervene on the *if* level in cases of unwelcome *then* effects.

The actual objects of fear are not NSA or Big Brother but *predictive analytics* and *algorithmic regulation*. They are kindred spirits of the *technocratic rationality* that was once discussed critically as the dark side of the Enlightenment under the headings of "reification" and "lack of responsibility." In the wake of big-data mining the dangers of technocratic rationality reveal themselves imminently as promoting an increasingly statistical view of society. We need a discussion that goes far beyond concerns over restoring the security of e-mail communication—as the chief replacement for a legally and physically inviolable postal system—in the face of digitization and global terrorism. The larger question pertains to the image modern society has of itself and how willing society is to allow its data scientists and their technologies to reshape it.

Daily journalism aside, discussions show that developments in the philosophy of science also support the paradigm of data mining in parallel to these problems of surveillance and privacy. With statistically determinable knowledge in clear view, the "end of theory" has been declared, and even the humanities strive to become "hard" science by generating quantitatively attested "knowledge." This shift from the subjective, from the ambivalence of interpretation, toward algorithmic methods of analysis, fulfills itself in a vision of "semantic publishing," formalizing statements into units that can be isolated autonomously, like entries in a database. From cultural studies' point of view, we see just how far away we have moved from Humboldt's educational ideals and from Lessing's conception of knowledge, one that discovered the purpose of mankind not so much in finding and managing the truth as in the process of searching for it.

The question worrying many of those who are concerned with the cultural effects of the present technological development is this: What possibilities does the individual have to intervene in this process? The answer must begin with the recognition that we do not speak for the majority. As long, for example, as Google is able to present itself as the eyes of God in the sense of caring rather than overseeing and judging, then any protest against big-data mining will raise objections from all those people who benefit from Google's "care." The debate on surveillance and privacy, instigated by the NSA scandal, ignores this general complicity and agreement. We do want Google to know everything about us so that it can fulfill its customer care as effectively as possible—from personalized search results via geolocal recommendations to suggestions as to what we should do next. We agree that the *smart things* in the Internet can only make our tasks easier to the extent to which they—and thus all who have access to their data—know about us.

Disciplining the various intelligence agencies is the only common denominator upon which society can still partway agree. And not even in this case is everyone of one mind. One needs to ask why people as citizens insist on a private sphere that they blithely ignore as consumers. In this context, those who call for the rescue of the Internet insofar as it is abused as a means of surveillance rightfully remind us of the hopes that were once associated with this new medium as a locus of emancipation and democratization. They also echo the intellectuals, today derided or forgotten, who back in the 1960s and 1970s called for the improvement of society, admonishing the disinterested people: There is no right life in the midst of a wrong one.

Changing media is even harder than changing societies. Apart from the social realm from which they emerge, media have their own inherent agenda that they are determined to fulfill. With respect to computers and the Internet this implies calculating, connecting, regulating. Big-data mining is not a byproduct of media development; it is its logical consequence. It radicalizes the Enlightenment impulse for mapping and measuring, something that today is inevitable and unavoidable because anything that happens digitally will produce data. Data analysis—regardless of any particular regime of data protection that may be in place—is not a "car accident" on the data highway; it is the actual destination. Data love—our love for data and its love for us—is the embrace that hardly anyone in this day and age can avoid. The forms it will take, what cultural and social side effects it will produce, and the ideas and reflections one can have about it from the perspective of philosophy or cultural studies are the subject of this book.

DATA LOVE

PART I

BEYOND THE
NSA DEBATE

1

INTELLIGENCE AGENCY LOGIC

I N the summer of 2013 the twenty-nine-year-old IT specialist Edward Snowden flew into a foreign country carrying with him secret documents produced by his employer, the National Security Agency of the United States (NSA). From the transit zone of the Moscow airport and with the help of the *Guardian* and the *Washington Post*, he informed the world about the extent of the surveillance of telephone and Internet communications undertaken by American intelligence agencies. In doing this, the whistleblower Snowden became much more successful than Thomas Drake, a former department head at the NSA who, with the same motives, had criticized the excessive surveillance practices of the NSA first through official channels and then in 2010 by divulging information to a journalist from the *Baltimore Sun*, for which he was later accused of espionage. Snowden's disclosures triggered an international sensation lasting many months, creating what historians at the time characterized as the last great epiphany to be experienced by media society.

This is how a report on the events of the NSA scandal of 2013 might begin in some distant future. The report would evaluate the event from a respectful historical distance and without the excitement or disappointment of earlier historians. From the distant future, this moment of revelation would prove to have been the last outcry before the realization that there were no alternatives to certain unstoppable technological, political, and social developments. The report from the future would reconstruct the case with historical objectivity, beginning by explaining how world leaders reacted.

The United States declares Snowden's passport invalid and issues a warrant of arrest for the breach of secrecy and theft. The Brazilian president protests at the United Nations over spying on Brazilian citizens (including herself). She cancels her planned meeting with the president of the United States and by creating an investigative committee again proves her capacity to act after the traumatic experience of the "#vemprarua" upheavals in her own country. Ecuador— its embassy in London housing the founder of WikiLeaks, Julian Assange—offers asylum to Snowden, thereby forgoing U.S. customs benefits. Germany denies Snowden's request for asylum on the technicality that one cannot file an application from a foreign country. Russia grants asylum to Snowden for one year, provoking a further cooling of its relations with the United States and immediately causing the cancellation of a planned summit meeting between Obama and Putin.

Net theoreticians appreciated Snowden's act because it forced society to debate matters that were long overdue for discussion. But acclaim did not come only from this quarter. Peer Steinbrück, the Social Democratic Party's candidate for the chancellorship of Germany, and the European Union's commissioner of justice, Viviane Reding, thanked Snowden for his civil courage and the debate he initiated.[1] Even a former president of the United States, Jimmy Carter, supported Snowden. The state's invasion of the private sphere, he claimed, had been excessive, and Snowden's disclosure would in all likelihood prove useful in the long run.[2] The current president remained inflexible in his thinking, although at a White House press conference on August 11, 2013, he conceded that the work of the NSA had to be more transparent. He announced that a commissioner for data protection would be appointed. But President Obama was vehemently opposed to the idea that Snowden should be treated as a patriot and not as a traitor: "No, I don't think Mr. Snowden was a patriot. I called for a thorough review of our surveillance operations before Mr. Snowden made these leaks. My preference, and I think the American people's preference, would have been for a lawful, orderly examination of these laws." Even if it were the case that Obama was a step ahead of Snowden, there's no denying that Snowden's act accorded with the impetus of Obama's review. Nonetheless, Snowden's nomination for the Nobel Peace Prize in 2014 underlines how different the reactions to Snowden's "treason" have been, especially when it comes to assessing the effect of his act on the world order.

The disclosures and accusations did not implicate the NSA alone. The British intelligence agency was also involved, and, as was later discovered, the German Federal Intelligence Service was working closely with the NSA, which should not have surprised anyone since, after all, a part of the September 11, 2001, team of assassins had come from Hamburg. It was generally known and widely accepted that this catastrophic event had justified many governmental data breaches and restrictions of civil liberties in the new millennium. The belief that defense against international terrorism inevitably requires limits on data protection was shared by the Obama administration and many other politicians. Even moral philosophers agreed. Peter Singer, for example, valued the gain in security over the loss of privacy in his essay "The Visible Man: Ethics in a World Without Secrets" (2011) since he considered privacy a recent, chiefly Western phenomenon in the history of mankind, one whose importance he relativized. It was particularly easy at the time, our future report might conclude, to smooth the way for the transition from a democratic society to a surveillance state by way of fear and "prudence."

If the future report were written by a German, it might at this point possibly refer to Christian Heller, who, simultaneously with Singer but independently, had published a sort of guide to the inevitable in his 2011 book *Post-Privacy. Prima leben ohne Privatsphäre* (Post-privacy. How to live well without a private sphere). Heller, the future report may then state, overcame the historical trauma of surveillance that has haunted German collective memory since the Third Reich and then the German Democratic Republic. It is possible that the report would regard Heller's book as igniting the spark for "the transparent 90 percent," the late 2010s citizen's movement that demanded more intensive security controls and attracted more and more followers. With their slogan "we have nothing to hide," they refused to risk their own lives for a minority's excessive adherence to privacy. The report would show how the followers of this movement proudly repudiated any kind of encryption in their digital communications, how they voluntarily installed the federal government's Trojan software on their computers and mobile devices, and how they were rewarded in return with VIP biometric security passes that granted them the use of special airplanes, subways, and buses.

No matter how these reports from the future would conclude, such a civil movement could be counted on to subscribe to statements such as the one from the German secretary of the interior at the time, Hans-Peter Friedrich of the Christian Social Union, who maintained that security is a "superfundamental right," or like the one by the former secretary of the interior, Otto Schily, the "red sheriff" of the Social Democratic Party, who declared that law and order are social-democratic values and that the biggest danger does not come from the state and its intelligence agencies but from terrorism and organized crime.[3]

Secretaries of the interior are, by nature, partisans of the work of their intelligence agencies, over and above party-political lines. After all, the government issued the mandates for which these agencies are now being publicly scolded, namely, to ward off threats to the inner security of their countries by way of the undercover investigations of possible risks. As Friedrich said in the context of the NSA affair, nobody should be astonished or upset when intelligence agencies use the latest cutting-edge technologies. Intelligence agencies want to secure and enhance their effectiveness just as much as any other functional social system; whatever is technologically possible will be used. For this reason, ever since 9/11 intelligence agencies had been dreaming of the "full take" of all data from all citizens. What had failed to materialize until then, because of financial and technological shortcomings, became a real option with the increasing digitization of society. The consensus was that those who did not use the new possibilities for data collection and evaluation were refusing to work properly, which in this realm of work might almost be regarded as treason.

It is obvious that the situation after 9/11 cannot be compared with that under the Stasi in former German Democratic Republic. In the Federal Republic of Germany the intelligence agency is constitutionally legitimized and controlled by parliament, even if not all members of parliament see it this way and continue to demand more transparency. The stronger argument is a technical one: Surveillance is no longer done by an intelligence agent who scrutinizes the letters and conversations of an individual but by software that searches for certain key terms. Even though the surveillance is more all-encompassing because of its use of modern technologies, it is also more anonymous and more democratic because it is not aimed at specific individuals but at all of society, including the intelligence agent himself. One could regard this as the perfect solution to an internal contradiction within every democracy: As the work of intelligence agencies becomes more and more effective and cost efficient, the private sphere of citizens is increasingly protected by the machinery of such "distant reading."

2

DOUBLE INDIFFERENCE

THE snooping around by the NSA and the support it received from other intelligence agencies was not the most scandalous aspect of the NSA affair. The real scandal lay in the helplessness of politics and the disinterest it revealed. The German president, who, as the former head of the Federal Commission on Stasi Affairs, should have been particularly sensitized regarding this subject, did not speak up at all. The chancellor spoke of the Internet as a "new territory for us all" and assured the public that on German soil German law has to prevail, as if the Internet could be bound to national laws by way of an increased insistence from the executive powers. The Social Democrats demanded complete clarification, as if they had nothing to do with setting the course for effective collaboration with the NSA and for a law on data retention during their own time in government. Others urged citizens to secure their own data more responsibly, as if it concerned only data presented voluntarily on Facebook and Twitter, as if all was well again as soon as cookies were blocked, e-mails encrypted, and the browser archive deleted every evening. Hardly any apps are at the disposal of those who are worried about their data since terms of use are not up for negotiation; apps triumphantly appear in the hard core of "take it or leave it." Protecting one's own data in this case means forgoing the use of a multitude of helpful, interesting, and simply entertaining programs. Perhaps there are a few everyday heroes who stubbornly refuse to click on "accept" if they feel that the appetite of an app for user and usage data is too great, but those who do this consistently must then ask themselves why they even own a smart phone if they use it only to make phone calls.

Nevertheless, at the time, the ignorance of the bulk of the population was scandalous. Even though a few folks demonstrated against the intelligence agencies' surveillance, the reaction did not measure up to the seriousness of the incident, which some even labeled a "digital Fukushima."[1] Most of those who were against surveillance still didn't do anything against it, saying that they had nothing to hide anyway. This gesture of appeasement is not only naive; it is also immoral, as can be seen from a concurrent newscast reporting on the marriage of two men in a Protestant church. Still forbidden by law and frowned upon several decades ago, this was now accepted by society and even consecrated by the church. In other words, from today's perspective, many people who had something to hide in the past—including those from the less recent past, such as doctors illegally dissecting corpses—had never been bad to begin with.

Those who advocate transparency across the board risk allying themselves with prevailing moral norms against the claims of minorities—or of new scientific findings, for that matter. In a democratic society that is aware of the partially backward-looking nature of its written and unwritten laws, it should be the duty of all citizens—a "superfundamental duty"—to protect the right to anonymity by practicing it themselves. This is the only way to cancel out the prospect that in the future everyone will be under suspicion if they attempt to evade outside control of their behavior—even if only by turning off their GPS. Considering that the laws of a democracy can never be either state of the art or carved in stone, this deserves serious reflection. Germany's history presents a frightening example. At a certain time in the past German citizens treated their data openly and did not conceal their Jewish ancestry, having no idea that this would lead to their deaths. How are we to know today which part of our "harmless" data will at some point be turned against us under future power structures?

In the present circumstances the statement "I have nothing to hide" is naive. Even if we don't care whether our GPS data will divulge with whom and where we have spent the night, we should not assume that others cannot figure us out better than we can ourselves. People are more than the sum of their data. Hidden insights are discovered in the digital summary and in comparisons, in the insights gained from statistics, and in the recognition of behavioral patterns. A famous, often-quoted example is that of the father from Minneapolis who complained to the retailer Target over the ads for baby products being sent to his underage daughter. Target had assumed her to be pregnant because the purchasing behavior of this woman had corresponded to the statistically generated consumption patterns of pregnant women. As it turned out, Target actually did know more about its customer than the father did about his daughter. What seems harmless to the initiator of an informationally implicated transaction—ordering a book from Amazon, commenting on YouTube, searching for certain terms through Google, or just buying certain articles—is a piece in the puzzle of a complex profile for big-data analysts, a profile that can tell them more about us than we know or want to know about ourselves. The algorithm is the psychoanalyst of the twenty-first century, delineating patterns of behavior that had previously remained hidden. The sales pitch for the Nike+ iPod Sport kit with pedometer is formulated precisely along these lines: "See all your activity in rich graphs and charts. Spot trends, get insights and discover things about yourself you never knew before."[2] How is it possible to exercise our basic rights to informational self-determination when the analyst brings things to light of which we weren't ourselves aware, all without asking us whether we permit the use of this information somewhere else or not?

No matter how one might assess or evaluate sensitivity to the breach of privacy in the population, suggestions for averting such breaches not only cited national and European laws against the media colonization of the United States but also made use of European technologies.[3] One response was an initiative by the German instant-messenger provider Whistle.im that promised—

in contrast and in response to the data-hungry WhatsApp—end-to-end encryption along with an allusion to German workmanship: "Secure Instant Messaging. Made in Germany" was their slogan. National regulation as a selling point for marketing on the Internet—what a change vis-à-vis the former animosity against state institutions! And how self-confidently and unceremoniously Perry Barlow's *Declaration of the Independence of Cyberspace* (1996) stated it at the time: "Governments of the Industrial World, you weary giants of flesh and steel, I come from Cyberspace, the new home of Mind. On behalf of the future, I ask you of the past to leave us alone." Whereas now we were hoping for help from the good old nation-state against the corporations of Silicon Valley.

Of course the subject was not a new one. For a long time the Internet has been discussed as a form of neocolonialism because by way of the Internet Western technophilia and its forms of communication have come into their own worldwide. And so the tedium of "downtime," which had hardly existed before and outside of the "carpe diem" dogma, becomes a lifestyle disease everywhere else because of our permanent communication over mobile media. Communities that in traditionalist cultures had the authority to determine the individual's life are all of a sudden confronted with flexible concepts of friendship in social networks.[4] In the context of the NSA debate, the media's neocolonialism is now also internal to the Western world, for example, as structuring conflicts between German culture and American technologies. But the lines of conflict are only seemingly aligned with national values; it is mainly the "digital immigrants" for whom German technologies with German data-protection laws are precious. The majority of the digital "natives" will continue using WhatsApp and will possibly do so more than ever since the transparency-apostle and data-octopus Facebook bought the company at the beginning of 2014 for nineteen billion dollars. What is treated as colonization is in fact fundamentally a generational conflict.

It is no surprise that despite this "intranational" tension the public debate remained focused on its international dimensions, chiefly discussing the extent to which the NSA was investigating the data of German citizens on German soil. Nation-states are better able to position themselves against another nation-state than against a technology operating globally and virally. When new disclosures and more memorable images—like the mobile phone of the German chancellor or the American "center of espionage" in the heart of Germany's capital—brought the NSA debate back onto the political agenda and eventually led to a special meeting of parliament, the discussion limited itself to the problem of Germany's sovereignty vis-à-vis the United States. This certainly is an important subject—just as important as the question of parliamentary control of the intelligence agencies and the propriety of its procedures. However, the essential debate—the radical digitization of society, practiced daily by increasing cohorts of chiefly digital natives—was thereby evaded.

3

SELF-TRACKING AND
SMART THINGS

WHEN the net critic Evgeny Morozov calls the American spies "dataholics" in a commentary on the NSA affair, demanding that they be committed to a "big data rehab" clinic, this represents a merely rhetorical gambit that he himself relativizes in the course of his article.[1] Morozov knows all too well that Russia, Snowden's sanctuary, loves, in this instance, the traitor more than the betrayal. After all, the criticism leveled against the NSA applies equally to the Russian intelligence agency, a fact that Morozov himself has addressed in the chapter "Why the KGB Wants You to Join Facebook," from his 2011 book *The Net Delusion: The Dark Side of Internet Freedom*. Yet it is not only the intelligence agencies that are addicted to limitless data love. Their coveting of "complete capture" finds its parallel—and here precisely lies the paradox of a possible reconciliation between society and its intelligence agencies—within society itself not only in the form of the widespread endorsement of smart things but also in what has come to be known as the self-tracking movement.

Commonly also referred to as the "quantified self," the culture of self-tracking has been developing for years, generating products like Fitbit, Digfit, Jawbone's Wristband, and Nike+, which monitor—and thereby control—the frequency of steps and pulse and thus also how we move, sleep, and eat. The imperative of absolute transparency is changing its character, promising that control will lead to self-awareness. Initially, it is striking to what extent the discourse of self-tracking is self-deluding in its populist form. The slogan connecting self-observation and self-optimization is "If you can measure it, you can learn to improve it."[2] Another slogan admits to the connection between technology and control ("If you can measure it, someone will . . .") but suggests that being proactive (". . . and that someone should be you") offers reassurance and benefit.[3] Of course one does not keep one's sovereignty over personal data by measuring oneself and by feeding the results into the system on the server of the provider. Instead, the statement underlines what Zygmunt Bauman has described as a "second managerial revolution" in claiming that the observation of man is taken over by the individual him- or herself, discipline replaced by self-discipline.[4] It is equally misleading when self-trackers cast themselves as in the "Know Thyself" tradition of the Oracle of Delphi,[5] which regarded self-knowledge as the recognition of one's own imperfections and limitations and which categorically did not mean an optimized "living by numbers."

Beyond the immediate goals of self-optimizing, self-tracking could be described as unconditional data love. Like any true love it promises no financial gain, nor does it have a reasonable goal. What a young self-tracker "who tracks everything from his mercury levels to his vitamin D consumption" announced in 2008 also holds true for others today, and even more so: "There's so much info that it'd be a shame not to track it."[6] To stay with the metaphor, true love surmounts the conventions of rationality and burns for the answers to far-fetched questions, like whether one falls asleep more quickly when standing on both legs for several minutes beforehand or how often one is typing each letter of the alphabet on one's keyboard.[7]

Nevertheless, the notion that self-trackers love data more than they love themselves would be presumptuous. The "unconditional" love for data of any kind is characterized by aspiration for a subsequent rationalization when new scientific methods create important insights from seemingly useless data about the producers of this data and thus society itself. This "unconditional" love, this aspiration for scientific insights, indicates that the undeniable obsession of self-trackers is not pure narcissism. Their data fetishism contains a social component that is initially expressed by making their personal data public and in helping others— fellow citizens, sociologists, physicians, traffic planners, and so on— understand people and society better.[8] From this perspective self-trackers are the avant-garde of an extraacademic self-study. They produce contextual, problem-oriented knowledge beyond the existing hierarchies of knowledge creation, thereby modifying the relationship between the sciences and society and echoing the statements of sociologists of knowledge since the beginning of the century. While in the course of modernity it has always been science that has spoken to society, now society "responds" to science in the guise of "lay experts."[9]

Smart things and the Internet of things provide another way of reconciling intelligence agencies with their citizens. This mantra was also cited by Morozov and others during the debate on data protection and privacy in the wake of the NSA scandal, but it hardly had the chance to gain ground against new disclosures, personal tragedy, and smashed hard disks. Yet the scenario of software-enabled everyday objects communicating with one another in order to reach programmatic decisions would have the potential for generating fascinating media spectacles: the swimming pool that heats up because a barbecue has been entered into the calendar, the fridge placing an order with the supermarket when the milk has reached its expiration date, the GPS that is aware of traffic jams and construction and automatically alters the car's itinerary. The Internet of smart things frees human intelligence from the menial tasks of analyzing situations with procedural consequences because the computer can do this work much faster and much more reliably. This is our liberation, freeing us to pursue higher goals, as the enthusiastic promise reads, but with, today, no clues as to where we might look for these goals.

At the same time, we are paralyzed by this very liberation. Marshall McLuhan, one of the founders of media studies, once upon a time called media "extensions of man": the elongation of arms (hammer, pistol), of legs (bicycle, car), of eyes (binoculars, microscope), and of memory (writing, photography). With the Internet of things, the computer now not only takes over calculation but also the observation and analysis of our environment (reasoning). For McLuhan, the dark side of the extension of organs was also an amputation because the advent of script does not train our memory any more than our legs develop muscles while we are driving. With the Internet of things a new amputation takes place, namely that of privacy. Not only do smart things cause our reasoning to atrophy, but they do so in the process of assimilating all possible personal data about us. If we don't feed them, they cannot serve us. The pool will remain cold when we don't allow it to see our calendar; GPS hardly helps when we don't tell it our destination. Smart things can only communicate to one another what they know about us, and if their service is based on intimate knowledge, then the breach of privacy happens for the sake of efficiency rather than control.

On this basis we will give these services—global players on the Internet—the very data that we don't want our intelligence agencies to have. As things stand, most of us find it a promise rather than a threat that Google is always attempting to improve the categorization of our situation, interests, and whereabouts so that at any time it can feed us recommendations about restaurants, shops, places of interest, and potential spouses in our vicinity. With the prospect of more efficient information management even a blatant technology of surveillance such as Google Glass may finally become socially acceptable. The problem of surveillance is not a political or economical one, although it is that as well; it is first a technological, philosophical, and anthropological one. Morozov calls it the "ideology of 'information consumerism.'"[10] This ideology—and this is the real scandal—surpassed the reach of the intelligence agencies by embracing everyone.

4

ECOLOGICAL DATA DISASTER

FUTURE history "books" will report that the paradigm change from a culture of personal privacy to one enforcing the absolute transparency of individual life was put into effect not only under the banner of measurement but also under that of networking. One will read that in the twenty-first century, the Internet of things inaugurated the triumph of artificial intelligence, given human complacency, over the remaining attempts at data protection. It consolidated objects and activities and simplified people's lives by way of control. Its immense accumulation of data was a paradise for all those interested in human behavior on a grand scale: sociologists, advertising experts, insurance companies, physicians, traffic and urban planners, law enforcement, and other agencies of security. Although the process was occasionally troubled by data protectors, for a long time the vast majority of the population had already been cooperating with the state and commercial data collectors. The majority had permitted a glimpse into its buying behavior via the supermarket discount card, and it was now "selling" its digital communication—or, rather, just giving it away, considering the value generated by the data for others. It was doing so, in fact, not only to get free Internet service; one didn't want to do without GPS either, not even when it began to cost more. Even Google Glass was, eventually, a great success, maybe because it gave everyone a place at the heart of a personal surveillance center in which one forgot that this technology had been set up chiefly in order to survey surveillance. At some point most people had acquired an "intelligent trash container" that although it no longer worked under the banner of self-optimization or information management was nonetheless serving governmental control by registering whatever was being tossed into it and notifying the town hall as to whether recycling was being done correctly.[1]

Future historians will identify the precursors of this development and use them to justify the status quo. They will refer to the Dutchman Alex van Es, an early-adopting pioneer of self-tracking who, in 1998, had already published the contents of his trash bin on the website icepick.com using a barcode scanner, proving that no obsession with data mining can be so absurd as not to be converted instantly into a business plan. One will immediately be reminded that the idea of surveillance had already been contemplated by the avant-garde artist Fernand Léger for a film that was to record twenty-four hours in the everyday life of a man and a woman without their knowledge (1931), as well as in Dan Graham's project *Alteration of a Suburban House* (1978), which was to replace the wall of a home with glass and thus bring the life of this family onto the neighborhood stage—both ideas quite some time before Peter Weir's *The Truman Show* (1998). These predecessors demonstrate the extent to which art, commerce, and control are interconnected. Future historians will also report that users of the intelligent trash container—which became generally accepted in the 2020s—received a discount on the cost of their garbage disposal and that "the transparent 90 percent" movement filed an application to revoke the security passes for anyone in a household that refused to participate in the "Smart Bin, Safer City" program.

On the background of these cultural-historical findings one might agree with Morozov that the commercialization of data cannot be prohibited by law as long as it is driven by the wishes of the people. Thus the debate in the wake of Snowden's disclosures revolved, instead, around questions of how to prevent Internet companies and intelligence agencies from collaborating. Morozov called this the reaching for the "low-hanging fruit,"[2] a political maneuver predicated on the delusion that one could keep state institutions from accessing commercially collected data. It is difficult to believe that politicians would allow this self-disempowerment vis-à-vis the commercial realm. After all, the state's intimate knowledge of the life of its citizens guarantees a more efficient fulfillment of its duties: lowering the cost of healthcare by detecting disease patterns early and introducing preventive care in cases of clearly detrimental behaviors, fighting against tax evasion and fraudulent social-security benefits through detailed knowledge of its citizens' buying habits, improving control of traffic flow by analyzing patterns of mobility, allowing for better city planning through a more accurate knowledge of spatial use, more efficiently managing energy by analyzing consumption profiles, and optimizing educational policy by gathering insight into individual patterns of interest and behavior.

No state will have any objection to knowing more about its citizens. On the contrary, every state will want to put at its disposal the data generated both through commercial and ideological tracking and data mining. Just how little can be expected from governments regarding data protection became clear on June 28, 2012, when the German Bundestag passed new legislation allowing the state to sell its citizens' data to advertising and credit agencies as long as citizens did not opt out by filing an objection. This resolution was made in an almost empty parliament as the twenty-first item of its agenda, shortly before 9 p.m., just after the beginning of the European Cup semifinals, Germany vs. Italy. The vote passed by a narrow margin but was later annulled following the protest of data protectionists. However, the fact that a majority of two or three politicians can pass such a law does not leave much room for consolation.

Is privacy better protected in the world of business? We might suppose so, given that its primary goal is not control or moral judgment but selling, satisfying whatever demand it perceives. However, for this very reason business is even more inquisitive than intelligence agencies, which are only concerned with potential threats. The transparent customer is the larger and weightier twin of the transparent citizen. Marketing consultants dream of the "full take" just as profoundly as intelligence agencies—if not more so—and of the real-time mining of social media, online communication, and offline actions. Among other things, they dream of the supermarket equipped with intelligent path tracking, that is, how a customer navigates the store based on data captured from their mobile. Via RFID chips feeding and coordinating biometric data the "smart" supermarket also registers, for example, whether a customer puts cream cheese back onto the shelf and opts for low-fat cottage cheese instead. Knowing his or her preference, the supermarket will now highlight diet products as the customer walks by and will also adjust in real time, assuming his willingness to pay more for less fat, the prices on the electronic displays.[3] Marketing loves data retrieval that allows for the refinement of the classical concept of segmentation as customization for the individual consumer.

The transparent customer is always also a transparent citizen. This justifies Morozov's concern that companies could be forced by governments to share their data. Morozov demands more than legislation in order to control IT companies. He maintains that it is necessary to take action to prevent a "data catastrophe" comparable to that envisaged by the ecological movement. At a certain point one's energy bill was no longer simply a private matter since the ecological consequences of individual energy consumption affects everyone. Analogously, our dealings in personal data have a public ethical dimension. Morozov is not only targeting the extrospective variant of self-tracking, that is, the saving and sharing of data that directly affects others (via camera, audio recording, or tagging in social media). Already the introspective variety—the gathering of personal data by insurance companies concerning driving or consumption habits, physical exercise, movement and mobility, and so on—presents a problem. It contributes to the determination of statistical criteria and norms against which all customers, regardless of their willingness to disclose private data, will be measured. Every purchase of an intelligent trash container increases the pressure on all those who do not yet cooperate with the data-collecting servants of the municipal garbage collector. Morozov's cautionary conclusion is that individual generosity—or perhaps promiscuity—with data sets the standards from which others will be unable to extricate themselves.

Morozov's perspective approaches the "ethics of responsibility for distant contingencies" demanded by Hans Jonas in his 1979 book *The Imperative of Responsibility: In Search of an Ethics for the Technological Age*. We have to consider the consequences of our actions even though they do not affect us or our immediate environment directly.[4] At the same time, Morozov's perspective points to the problem of surveillance, underlining just how complex the subject is as soon as one delves into it more deeply.[5] This approach turns the victims themselves into perpetrators while signaling the inefficacy of legal action vis-à-vis more complex and ambivalent ethical discussion. No wonder that others have pointedly recast Morozov's intimation of a structural problem within information society as a matter of politics. Among the reactions to Morozov's contribution in the *Frankfurter Allgemeine Zeitung* one could read that total surveillance is an insult to democracy, that mature citizens were being treated like immature children, and that the protest should not be seen in terms of the ecological movement but rather as comparable to the 1960s resistance against "emergency legislation." The political inflection of discussion was echoed in the appeal of Gerhart Baum, the former interior secretary from the Free Democratic Party: "We lack a citizen's movement for the protection of privacy as it existed and exists for the protection of natural resources."[6] Only the late chief editor of the *Frankfurter Allgemeine Zeitung* Frank Schirrmacher noted—and more than once—that the general sense of alarm in the wake of Snowden's revelations did not result from the disclosure of sophisticated surveillance technologies but from the realization that those technologies apply the same logic, systems, formulas, and mechanisms that determine our everyday life and working environment. Elsewhere, Schirrmacher, speaking about GPS, points out that the intercommunication of the giants of Silicon Valley and the intelligence agencies has not come about in a dystopian, Orwellian mode but "by way of things that even please us."[7] This fusion between what we fear and what we desire is the problem that paralyzes politics and people.

Morozov's correlation of environmental and data catastrophe, which meanwhile has gained some notoriety, is, in the end, unsound. When speaking of data catastrophe, the principle of a shifting baseline—as used in the discourse of the environmental catastrophe—is not equivalent to the destruction of the natural resources for future generations. The data catastrophe "only" threatens current cultural norms, and by contrast with global warming and pollution, a disaster resulting from altered values applied to social coexistence is hardly guaranteed. While the ecological movement's call to halt in response to the looming end of mankind can hardly be contradicted (the focus of contention being only a matter of the urgency of its appeal), saying "Halt" to cultural change would seem to oblige future generations to observe established norms of social interaction.[8] When motivated by cultural concerns, an ethics of preservation is less convincing than when it is a response to the known threat of environmental catastrophe. Not only must a culturally inclined ethics of preservation substantiate the reality of a threat; it must also speak to its menacing character, all the while resisting the counterargument that radical upheavals of culture are inherent within modernity.

The data catastrophe demands a more profound discussion than that surrounding questions of how to retain the integrity and privacy of mail in the age of digitization. It points to a change of social mentalities chiefly embodied in digital natives. The fact that this constituency appears unbothered by the loss of their private sphere is for many—and especially for members of the older generation—evidence of ignorance and indifference. From a psychosociological perspective, the lack of protest might also be understood as an emancipatory effort—as a longing for a realm that no longer differentiates between the private and the public, or as a rebellion against parents and grandparents whose earlier cultural revolution, which involved—in the 1960s and 1970s—making the private sphere public, has now become further radicalized with the help of the new media. On the one hand, this rebellion may be seen as very successful, given all the complaints of the older generation concerning the youthful lack of concern. On the other hand, this longing may simply be a resurgence that can be referred back to historical models since, in the early twentieth century, transparent man was not only invoked by communists against bourgeois culture but also by the Western avant-garde.[9] The guiding principles of other earlier cultural tendencies—best expressed in Georg Simmel's declaration "The secret is one of man's greatest achievements" as well as in Peter Handke's admission "I live off of what the others don't know about me"[10]—lose their validity under the contemporary imperative of transparency and disclosure, to say nothing of the fact that they prove to be impracticable against the prospects of intelligent things and smart environments. From this perspective, surveillance and control are merely the social implementation of the radical transparency widely propagated and practiced in social networks.

Compared to the ecological catastrophe, as an existential problem the data catastrophe is less menacing and as an ethical one less unequivocal. It is possible that this is the reason that Morozov's discomforting but entirely necessary call for a larger debate to counteract our data-specific ignorance has proved ineffective. Perhaps it explains the appeal of the emancipated-citizen-versus-suppressive-state rhetoric, which was made all the more persuasive when the British government blundered in sending its Secret Intelligence Service to the *Guardian*'s offices in order to destroy the hard disks holding Snowden's information. With this purely symbolic act of power—no intelligence agency worthy of its name believes that in the age of digital reproduction unwanted data can be erased through material violence—the media circle was strategically closed at the point where it had begun, namely with Edward Snowden's "betrayal." Although many have rightly regarded this betrayal as more of an awakening and as a call to necessary debate, in most cases the discussion does not go beyond the consequences that Snowden himself attributed to his disclosures. It is easy to understand why.

5

COLD CIVIL WAR

THE hypothetical future report relating the events of the NSA affair and Snowden's betrayal will probably be ambivalent about listing Snowden among the heroes of history not because his deed was evaluated differently even by former U.S. presidents but because his purported heroism was based on a romantically glorified view of society. As Snowden declared in his interview with the *Guardian* in July 2013 and his TED talk in March 2014, he had wanted to inform the world about the snooping programs so that it would have the chance to do something to counteract it. He saw himself as a scout and trailblazer for change, someone with no doubt that his conscience would exonerate him for breaking any oaths of office that had been in the way of the truth. He believed in martyrdom, in giving up his own life for the public good. And indeed, Snowden is a contemporary version of the David and Goliath myth, attesting to the power of the individual in the face of the most powerful of nations, an example of the fact that, outside the academic system, certain discursive controversies can be launched and addressed with greater impact—something that critical scientists have been zealously working toward with little success.

The ambivalence of Snowden's heroism is not connected with his optimistic belief in the good of people but in its claim for some kind of ownership of the Internet. This gesture can be seen in the title of his TED talk: "Here Is How We Take Back the Internet." Who is talking? How many of *us* are there? How can they reserve the right to determine the fate of a medium? When we reduce the problem of data protection to the snooping of intelligence agencies, it may be plausible to demand restitution, and the questions above may appear to have obvious answers. But if one sees the "ideology of 'information consumerism,'" as Morozov puts it, as part of a social development, the question arises: Through what mandate—and with what chance of success—do activists wish to dictate the development of a medium that they do not own? To be clear, my question is aimed at the logic of the argument and in no way indicates any dismissal of the demands arising. On the contrary, the hope is that by addressing its cultural and social roots the problem will be tackled more rigorously. What renders Snowden's heroism critically ambivalent is the superficiality of the debates it has incited, sometimes even soliciting the help of those who have internalized the ideology of data consumption while preaching it with their products: the software developers and data miners.

We cannot exclude the possibility that some software developers will be sensitized by the discussion of data protection and will refrain from the unnecessary retrieval of user data when they program their next app. It is conceivable that privacy could be prized above the economic considerations of data accumulation. However, given the increasing role that big data is playing in the economy, one cannot expect many startups to abstain voluntarily from data mining—not unless the payoff manifests itself as a competitive advantage in the form of consumer preference. Here lies a potential that has been initiated by the debates. In the realm of digital media it is possible that a parallel market will develop that values the protection of customer data over the profit to be made from data capture. An "organic Internet," so to speak, whose products would be relatively more expensive, as are vegetables without pesticides and meat from happier chickens. Such a market might undermine, from an unexpected direction, the fiercely contested arguments for net neutrality—data transmission independent of form, content, sender, and the reputation or spending capacity of the receiver—possibly stirring net activists into more protests. The problems facing a two-class Internet, however, are not greater than those of the divided food market. On the contrary. With regard to food, the reasons some people decide to buy a less safe product are purely economic, whereas on the apps market the choice could also be made on the basis of conviction. In any case, the discussion will advance these economic and ideological questions instead of remaining stalled in the legal mire that Snowden has brought it to.

Limitations of the ongoing discussion are illustrated by a survey of ten "pioneers and theoreticians of the Internet" featured in the weekly newspaper *Die Zeit* on the question: "Can the Internet Be Saved?"[1] The answers are rife with militancy and only occasionally show any deeper awareness of the true problems. For example, Markus Beckedahl, the operator of the blog netzpolitik.org, writes: "Nothing less than our digital future with the basic values and rights that we know and have learned to love is at stake." And in a similar vein Anke Domscheit-Berg, a net activist and leading candidate of the Brandenburg Pirates Party in the governmental elections, urges: "We can continue pretending to be blind and deaf, and we will find ourselves in a world in which we will attempt to explain to our children that, at one time, there was a free Internet and how, when it ended, many other elements of freedom disappeared forever. But we can also powerfully revolt and reclaim with tooth and claw the Internet as we once knew it." Love, teeth, claws—an honorable protest against the course of events that nevertheless ignores the extent to which the early Internet carried its current structure within itself all along. The old aspiration—given up in the meantime by most net theoreticians—of the Internet as a place of free and liberating communication rested from the beginning on a misunderstanding; it is a misperception of the net as something existing independently of the computer. Advocates underlined all the possibilities of networking and overlooked the requirements of calculation that computation imposes on the human condition the more it provides links from computer to computer. Networked computers want to measure and calculate everything just as much as they want to copy everything. With regard to copying, the answer for many—and mainly for net activists—is to say goodbye to the copyright rules of the analog world. The same applies to privacy. Measuring and transparency are the end-all of the be-all. Here also clinging to past customs does not help.

In this light, Viktor Mayer-Schönberger, a coauthor of the book *Big Data: A Revolution That Will Transform How We Live, Work, and Think* (2013), answers in the same survey much more to the point and without illusions: "In a nutshell this is the new task of governments—the all-encompassing, provisional control of society, based on information. And yet, governments are late-comers. They follow businesses like Google and Facebook and organizations like Wikipedia (and WikiLeaks!) that have recognized this much earlier. This is not the end, this is only the beginning." Cybernetics—no teeth or claws will help here—has always been the cover-up for a control to which more and more aspects of human life are now subjected through the Internet—of both people and of things. It is obvious that governments will use these new affordances in order to fulfill their tasks more effectively, and the political discussion will hardly question this. In most cases it will insist only that data mining take place in a transparent and democratic way. The instruments of control should be visible (with the welcome side effect that self-disciplining will result), and they should be accessible to everyone (which, considering the true cost of complex data analysis, can hardly be realized).[2]

In his "Postscript on the Societies of Control" Gilles Deleuze illustrates a future city "where one would be able to leave one's apartment, one's street, one's neighbourhood, thanks to one's (dividual) electronic card that raises a given barrier." Twenty years later this prognosis has been realized in products like the NFC Ring, which opens locks, or the Nymi wristband, which uses one's personal pulse rate as a means of identification. At the same time, what for Deleuze is the dystopian aspect of his scenario is also realized: "but the card could just as easily be rejected on a given day or between certain hours; what counts is not the barrier but the computer that tracks each person's position—licit or illicit—and effects a universal modulation."[3] Despite knowing that IBM has created a control room in Rio de Janeiro in which the feeds from all surveillance cameras are concentrated or that China is building similar control rooms in its new cities, one should not paint the future with old conceptual brushes. In the end there will be no Big Brothers to be dragged out of their control centers. There will be no live controllers who will activate or deactivate the cards. These cards will obey algorithms fed by the all-but-limitless collections of data that we have ourselves given up freely. The term for this has already been coined: "algorithmic regulation." Its congenial genius is "datafication," the transformation of communications and activities into quantifiable, tabulated data. The transition from a society of discipline into one of control, as announced in political philosophy, is implemented through the digitization of society. Datafication guarantees its execution by way of cybernetics.

More than forty-five years ago another, older branch of political philosophy already revealed many problems of society's adaptation to the logic of cybernetics under the heading "technocratic rationality." Its perspective, supposedly, replaces the authoritarian state, which leads to an end of discursive controversy. The realization of a normative moral order, which is "a function of communicative action oriented to shared cultural meaning and presupposing the internalization of values," is "increasingly supplanted by conditional behavior."[4] Bourgeois and socialist ideology thus gives way to an ideology determined by technology and science as "self-reification of men under categories of purposive-rational action and adaptive behavior."[5] The problem—as elucidated by Jürgen Habermas expanding on Max Weber's and Herbert Marcuse's criticism of rationality—is the transformation of rationality itself from a means of emancipation for mankind into a means of its reification. Max Horkheimer and Theodor Adorno have described this aspect of the process of modernization in their *Dialectic of Enlightenment* (1944), and Zygmunt Bauman has dealt with it as "dialectic of order" in his *Modernity and the Holocaust* (1989). In each case, instrumental rationality—albeit with different levels of cruelty—creates a situation of "moral mercilessness" in which people no longer feel responsible for existing rules of behavior nor feel the need to challenge them; they simply follow and enforce them with an august sense of obligation. Adiaphorization—the technical term in ethics for when people do not feel responsible any longer for the effects of their actions—becomes redundant (or is hiding behind the interface) when it is no longer a person but the algorithm (as the new, perfect "brother Eichmann") who sets the rules and enforces them.

In a recent book on *Liquid Surveillance: A Conversation* (2012), Bauman pointed out the danger of outsourcing moral responsibility to technological developments: "We no longer develop techniques 'in order to' do what we want to be done, but we select things for doing just because the technology for doing them has been developed (or, rather, has been come across; accidentally—'serendipitously'—found)."[6] The question of where these technologies come from, supplying us with parameters of action, and of how the inventive spirit and the profit orientedness of young programmers cohere, will be discussed later. Let these following cautionary words—from a similar statement on the automatic link between technological possibility and practical usage in Hans Jonas's abovementioned book on responsibility—suffice for now. For Jonas the fate of man lies in the "triumph of *homo faber*," which makes him into "the compulsive executer of his capacity." As Jonas states: "If nothing succeeds like success, nothing also entraps like success."[7] We have given in to this technological success more than ever. The modern terms for this are computing, programming, deploying algorithms.

The submission to what is technologically possible—both trumpeted and deplored—also explains why there is such interest in analyzing the behavioral patterns of employees and how they communicate, with solutions offered by companies such as Sociometric Solutions, Hitachi, and Evolv. E-mail filters, data mining, sociometric badges, and other methods and devices that analyze internal company communications, cooperation, and movements may throw up red flags for union activists and privacy advocates. However, the aim of optimizing the working process in order to "develop a more productive, more positive and more profitable workforce" and "to drive increased employee satisfaction, retention, productivity and engagement"—which Evolv states as its mission—does not sound unreasonable. After all, how can you deny employers the right to know what their employees are doing during paid work time? But this may already be the wrong question. The fact is that they want to know as much as they can—as the software engineer Ellen Ullman illustrates in her 1997 *Close to the Machine: Technophilia and Its Discontents*. She recalls the owner of a small insurance business who wanted her to help him record all his office manager's keystrokes: "You can count every keystroke, and you want to count them simply because it's possible. You own the system, it's your data, you have power over it; and, once the system gives you this power, you suddenly can't help yourself from wanting more." Technology creates desire; its options are no option for us: "We think we are creating the system, but the system is also creating us. We build the system, we live in its midst, and we are changed."[8] Ullman's conclusion confirms Bauman's and Jonas's warnings that media have their own agenda. As previously stated in words usually attributed to the Canadian media theorist Marshall McLuhan: "We become what we behold. We shape our tools and then our tools shape us."

If, in the context of the NSA affair, placards blazoned with "YES WE SCAN" appeared in demonstrations during the summer of 2013, they were pointedly referring to President Obama's election slogan "YES WE CAN," expressing their disappointment in him and his policies. The conceptual and actual rhyme of these two slogans—we scan because we can—simultaneously articulates the fatalistic activism that for Jonas and Bauman characterizes the relationship of modernity and technology. Yes, we can collect all kinds of data, and we can analyze them—and therefore we do it. The "full take" that the intelligence agencies are aiming for is no contradiction in modern society; it is a part of its inherent contradictory nature. Control society and the *Culture of Control*—the title of a 2001 book by David Garland—are the consequences of processes of modernization that, if nothing else, apply all available technologies to improve ever more effective methods of organization and control.

The contradictory nature of the modern era has also ensnared its powerless populations. Pragmatic considerations have led to an unsolicited provision of data simply for the sake of comfort and the thirst of knowledge, as can be seen from the example of contemporary human interaction with self-tracking and smart things. During the NSA scandal one could observe that the lack of protest might be explained differently. This lack was a function of a "longing for surveillance" in the sense of being taken care of or looked over in a modern world that has become confusing, and also of a "*love* of being seen" in the sense of "I am seen (watched, noted, recorded), therefore I am."[9] Both motives—exhibitionism as self-assurance and the desire for order as a reduction of complexity—are psychologically comprehensible—as is the thirst for knowledge and comfort. Potentially, this makes the individual into an ally of monitoring and control.

When, also in the context of the NSA affair, there is talk of a "cold civil war,"[10] the conflict should not be seen as reducible to one between citizen and state, or as a war between digital natives and digital immigrants, or between those who buy and sell data or illegitimately acquire data and all the others. The civil war is taking place not between the citizens but *within* each citizen, that is, between the interest in technological progress, orientation, and being noticed on the one hand and, on the other, the occasional sense of discomfort at being the object of surveillance and control. This internal civil war hinders all attempts at strengthening data protection through, for example, a system of decentralized data storage in individual routers and servers. Although this would weaken the data octopuses of the Internet by exploiting the Internet's fundamentally decentralized structure, it would also rob the citizenry of many advantages that are a result of the centralization and interconnection of data. The question that needs to be untangled is this: To what extent can modern society resist the allure of new inventions and the advantages that they promise?

If such resistance does not succeed, future histories may report on this dispute as follows: In 2023 the German Ministry of the Internet (MOTI), which had been created shortly after Snowden's disclosures, took out an injunction against the Association of Activists of Data Protection (AADP). Their so-called white block had long ago demanded—by referring to Gilles Deleuze and other critics of the cybernetic control society—the creation of "vacuoles of noncommunication" as "circuit breakers,"[11] an example being the deactivation of GPS tracking on smart phones. Although by 2023 it was no longer possible to deactivate GPS tracking, owning a smart phone with a "presence tag" was not yet mandatory. Changes were proposed by MOTI because the Department of Transportation was planning to require presence technology for traffic regulation (with a location precision of five centimeters). This was particularly important because by this time all driven vehicles were virtually soundless. Collisions could be avoided through this technology, even for the deaf or blind, by automatically triggering warning signals or braking commands for two presence-tag carriers whose locational coordinates fell below the distance limit. This technology, which was regarded as absolutely secure, could scarcely be refused by the data-protection activists, but they nevertheless demanded anonymization. After all, preventing a collision between a car and a bicycle, for example, did not require the identification of the drivers. The Ministry of the Internet did not share this point of view, reasoning that given the data available concerning the physical and psychological condition of the drivers, their everyday routines, the car models, and many other factors, state-of-the-art data mining could help calculate the probability of a collision and allow the enforcement of appropriate preventive measures in an even more timely manner. They argued that since traffic safety was not a private matter, no citizen should be allowed to remain anonymous in this instance. The demand to create barriers in the way of cybernetic communication was regarded as dangerous, and even as terroristic by some, and therefore it was forbidden by law.

PART II

PARADIGM CHANGE

6

DATA-MINING BUSINESS

HE society of the future will be a society of communicative capital. Anyone with a high degree of influence in forming opinions on social media will enjoy checking in as if they had booked business class; their rooms will be upgraded on arrival at the hotel, and they will be rewarded with perks in many other situations. "Perks" is the name given by the San Francisco startup Klout, founded in 2008, for the small extras that one receives, here and there, for a high "Klout score." The Klout score indicates a person's communicative importance, their "influence across several social networks," on a scale of 1 to 100. The score is calculated from more than four hundred signals, including the number of followers, retweets, comments, likes, friends on Facebook, the number of citations on the Internet, and backlinks to a personal website. In the end we arrive at a score that can be compared with all the others, something that Klout calls for explicitly on its Facebook site: "Invite your friends to compare your scores."[1]

A society that creates differentiations based on rankings and provides financial advantages based on communicative capital—which is close to social capital in Pierre Bourdieu's terms—appears as a better alternative relative to a society that operates chiefly on the basis of economic power. However, this understanding will change when, given viral marketing, communicative capital becomes firmly integrated in the business models of hotels and airlines and as communicative capital itself becomes commodified—through the purchase of Facebook friends and Twitter followers, for example. Whatever happens, it is an important sociological question demanding a wide-ranging critical discussion at least as soon as schoolchildren begin to select their friends, or companies their employees, based on Klout scores.

For the media theorist, the phenomenon of the Klout score directly addresses a fundamental question of the discipline: Does technology determine society, or vice-versa? Do computation and the Internet impose Klout scores on people, or do human practices make them inevitable? If society's guiding medium already carries the drive to calculate in its name, and if, given the digitization of almost all communication on the Internet, this medium has an ever-increasing amount of data on the behavior of individuals at its disposal, then everything seems to point in the direction of technological dominance. On the other hand, people's interest in statistics and ranking did not originate with the rise of the personal computer. A paradigm change from qualitative to quantitative understanding can already be found in the late Middle Ages.[2] In the contemporary public-management society that increasingly pursues its own rationalization—and even, for example, calculates the quality of scientific publications on the basis of citation indexes—the invention of an influence index in social networks is a logical consequence facilitated but not caused by computers and the Internet.

Regardless of how one answers this crucial question of media studies, one can hardly deny the prognosis: The society of the future will be one of data mining and number crunchers. Business analysts are now promoted as "data scientists"; statistics—once the domain of nitpickers—has become a profession with sex appeal. The super-crunchers are the superheroes of the twenty-first century, their names consistently popping up on the latest lists of up-and-coming millionaires.[3] The generation of Klout scores is not their most profitable activity, but it symbolizes perfectly the obsession with measurement within the "statistical turn" that accompanies the digitization of society.

The business of big-data mining is distinguished by three distinct modes of operative agency: Data owners who possess the data but do not analyze what they collect (Twitter), data specialists who help the data owners use their data most effectively through complex methods of analysis (Teradata, for Walmart), and businesses and individuals who gather information with original and unconventional perspectives or methods for which no one had yet thought of an application (FlightCaster.com predicting flight delays based on the analysis of ten years of data on flights and weather). The modes may overlap—for example, when MasterCard evaluates the accumulated data on the buying patterns of its customers and then sells its findings to advertisers—and business models can evolve: Credit-card issuers may in the future allow transfers of money free of charge in return for access to or analysis of more data that they can sell on. At the same time, new business models emerge from the possibilities for recombining and reusing data, examples being "data intermediaries" that utilize data acquired from different sources in an innovative way.[4]

The inevitable flip side of data love is an indifferent, if not hostile, relationship with the world of human privacy. At the precise point when data entrepreneurs dig into the vast depth and extent of the accumulated data in order to claim the treasure of a promising competitive advantage, petty, individual concerns of privacy will be in the way of their spirit of discovery, just as the aged couple Philemon and Baucis, in Goethe's *Faust*, stood in the way of modern-day business practices. An important part of big-data business is, therefore, the management of mood. The subjects or objects of the data—our choice of terminology depending on whether, for instance, one attributes the production of GPS data to the user of a mobile phone or to its provider—have to be convinced of the entrepreneurs' good intentions, namely, that their goal is to develop better products and to offer improved customer care, as the announcement of the Data Love conference declared. One has to convince the potential customer to see big-data mining as the great adventure of our times, an adventure in which everybody is obliged to participate. For, in contrast to former times, when courageous businessmen embarked on dangerous voyages, risking their lives for potential gains, the entrepreneurs of big-data business must take the entirety of society along for the ride.

At the same time, it should be stressed that it is not only business that may accrue profit from the data of their customers; customers can also profit from the data of businesses. A good example is the computer specialist Oren Etzioni, who reacted to the realization that he had paid more for his plane seat than his neighbors by creating the startup Farecast, a program that uses statistical analysis to predict variations in fares. Anyone who helps others to save money in such a way will, in the end, make money for himself—or as soon as his company, as happened with Farecast, is bought for 110 million dollars by Microsoft.[5] The story of Farecast points to the fact that data mining does not thrive on personalized advertisement alone; it shows that in an information society profit flows from the trade of information in general and that, quite naturally, it is made by those who are able to broker it.

7

SOCIAL ENGINEERS
WITHOUT A CAUSE

"**I**f you want to become a millionaire, you have to solve a hundred-million-dollar problem" is Silicon Valley's rule of thumb. What's up for grabs are the as-yet-overlooked niches in the data business, the so-far-untried methods for analyzing data, and the ideas that no one has yet thought of. However, more important than solving a problem is convincing someone in the Valley that the product offered is the solution to a problem no one knew existed. The contrast between responsive solutions and proactive, enforced solutions is illustrated by the comparison between Farecast, an airline-ticket-pricing app, and the Hapifork, a fork that records the frequency with which it is put to the mouth. The supervision of eating habits—evoking warnings when eating too fast—is, according to the startup Hapilabs, the answer to digestive problems, heartburn, and above all obesity. Since one only feels satiated twenty minutes after eating, eating too fast means eating too much.[1] Who would have thought that innovations were still possible in the fork market—the design of forks has always appeared to be as perfect as that of books! On the other hand, a fork is just a mindless piece of steel or plastic, and although the "intelligent fork" may have arrived too early for the taste of the masses, in the context of all the other tracking devices and smart things that measure and facilitate human existence, it could well be that soon we will find ourselves unable to live without it.

Of course, most of the money is still spent on solving real problems, even though, from the perspective of cultural philosophy, the solution itself might be the problem. A good example is the app Summly, which algorithmically recognizes the key terms of a text and distills its essence in four hundred characters. This is one way of responding positively to information overload: Instead of having to go on an information diet, one acquires a tool for processing even more information. Dieting is the solution for digital immigrants who would rather read less text with more accuracy. The impetus for digital natives is to process more texts faster, and that is why Summly has been so successful, making its programmer, Nick D'Aloisio, born in 1995, the richest teenager in the world after Yahoo bought the app in the spring of 2012 for thirty million dollars. The promise of the app is not only textual concision but also a method for learning more, faster because one doesn't have to search for the core message of a text oneself.[2] It is only possible to believe that Summly makes one smarter, as it suggests, if one translates "smart" not as "intelligent" but as "sly" or "crafty." It is indeed crafty to outsource information processing, which represents actual intelligence, to computing capacity.

While Summly is one contemporary strategic solution to a current problem, other apps in data mining validate themselves through historical means. Reading, for instance, is shifting away from being an intimate cultural practice and becoming a social interaction, as when Kindle readers see the highlighting of other readers within a text and are able to add their own, or when an app like Readmill shares collective opinions on readers' most beloved scenes. Social reading within digital media is reminiscent of book clubs in the later twentieth century and reading communities at the end of the eighteenth. The difference lies in the expansion and instrumentalization of the social aspect when one reads online, for now others too have access to the details of reading, others including those who may be uninterested in the books being read or in having any interaction with readers. These others' sole interest lies in tracking current reading habits in order to optimize future books and marketing strategies for the products of publishing: what is being read when, how fast, and how often; what is being marked, what skipped, which words are looked up, which facts are being googled.

Social reading could be seen as a corrective for hyperreading, as a return to reading more accurately by way of collective discussion. However, it should be considered that beyond the opportunistic rhetoric of transparency and interaction, these transparent readers are chiefly the representatives of commercial interests and requirements. Under the banner of product improvement texts are to be made more pleasing so as to meet the expectations and needs of the reading public—and the same will be true for film and video, given that their media businesses mine the viewing habits of millions of Netflix users, for example.[3] From the perspective of cultural philosophy, such market-driven customization is counterproductive. Here reading is also understood as a conflict between author and reader, or between director and viewer, for the predominance of a reality model. Readerships and audiences can only win this fight when they lose it, that is, when they learn to see reality from a different, from a new, perspective. This is not only true for the way in which one sees something but also for the way in which one describes it. Seen from the perspective of the Frankfurt School, this would translate to saying that the pleasing piece of art cheats the audience because it does not offer a resistance through which he or she is enabled to become more than he or she already is. The logic of this perspective claims that in the book or film market customer service should be aimed at denying short-term customer interests, that is, by *not* altering those passages that have proven to be resistant and obstinate in content or style but by reinforcing them.

However, this suggestion would not only violate big-data mining's free-enterprise logic; it would also misapprehend the social status quo, whose central interest is hardly humanity's exit from its self-imposed immaturity, as it may have been during the high point of the Enlightenment and bourgeois humanism or in the Marxist social model. In our current circumstances the book is hardly seen as a medium for individual emancipation, even by intellectuals.[4] The claim that self-development is in the interest of improving the world has long lost its political and philosophical credibility. Indeed, this loss of credibility was initially disguised, in the 1990s, by an Internet that seemed to offer a place of utopian and heterotopian promise. But during the subsequent commercialization and disciplined reorganization of the formerly "anarchic" medium, this hope was also lost. Under the banner of data love what remains is only the promise of knowledge discovery in databases or, depending on how one sees it, the dystopia of greater control.

Once a utopia of the social degenerates before the ideal of absolute measurement and efficient social administration, the protagonists of social change also change. The social engineers of the twenty-first century are no longer *hommes des lettres* with humanist ambitions. There are no longer writers to whom a Stalin dictates how they should reform the minds of the people. There are no longer artists expressing political guidance, nor political intellectuals who broach the subjects that society goes on to discuss. The social engineers of today are the software programmers, the number crunchers, and the widget producers who are changing human life stealthily but thoroughly with their analyses and applications; they are the graduates and dropouts of the computer and engineering sciences who influence future social values with startups like Klout and apps like Summly; they are the developers who are either unwilling or unable to judge the cultural implications of their technical inventions both because of the characteristics of their profession or simply because of their age: being young, many engineers have much less experience with the complex structures of social life and the contradictory demands of human existence. Even if they were to have something to say about the consequences of their inventions, they take refuge in a calculated optimism that regards technology as, intrinsically, an amelioration of the human situation, something that makes the world a better place, as the Silicon Valley mantra goes, or they delegate responsibility to the users and politicians, claiming that technology is neutral. Or they show a steadfast enthusiasm for the technical unknown. They may admit that new technology is not only full of promise but also comes with its perils, but they insist that it is, in any case, exciting, fascinating, and fantastic.

This willingness to take on risks, this blind embrace of change, represents a shift from the wariness of intellectuals toward the curiosity of inventors and entrepreneurs. What Hamlet in his famous soliloquy admits as a problem for thinkers is not necessarily a problem for tinkerers:

> Thus conscience does make cowards of us all,
> And thus the native hue of resolution
> Is sicklied o'er with the pale cast of thought,
> And enterprise of great pitch and moment
> With this regard their currents turn awry
> And lose the name of action.[5]

Such a shift in power is not without its forerunner: Francis Bacon had already imagined it in his social utopia *Nova Atlantis* in 1627. Here it is no longer the philosopher occupying the center of the ideal state (as in Plato's *Republic*, for example) but the scientist constructing social life on the basis of empiricism and rationalism. The data scientist and the programmer are the postmodern descendants of Bacon's scientists; however, their only plan for the world is that it must be programmable. These are social engineers with no convictions or agendas beyond "computationalism" and the "softwarization" of society.[6]

8

SILENT REVOLUTION

TALK of revolution is not only to be found in Mayer-Schönberger's and Cukier's book *Big Data*. The authors of the collection of essays *The Human Face of Big Data* also use the term liberally and go so far as to write, with no concern for possible objections, about the grandest upheaval in human history since the agrarian revolution ten thousand years ago.[1] For Eric Schmidt (formerly Google's CEO) and Jared Cohen (at present the director of the Google think tank Ideas) the Internet is "driving one of the most exciting social, cultural, and political transformations in history," a revolution that will influence "how we interact with others and how we view ourselves."[2] It should not seem surprising that the dystopian prospect of unavoidable and all-encompassing control of individuals hardly perturbs the authors. Their recipe for dealing with this is self-censorship and identity management. Avoid doing anything that could not be published before the court or on the front page of a newspaper. For everything else there will be identity managers with monthly reports and suggestions on how to optimize one's online persona. In addition—the book was written before the NSA debate—these authors were conjuring up a prestabilized harmony between citizens, state, and the economy: "People will share more than they're aware of. For governments and companies, this thriving data set is a gift, enabling them to better respond to citizen and customer concerns, to precisely target specific demographics of the population, and, with the emergent field of predictive analytics, to predict what the future will hold."[3]

It is evident that this perspective represents a different picture of society than that addressed by Adorno's critical theory, Foucault's surveillance society, or Deleuze's control society. Any perspective reflecting on power structures should be skeptical and suspicious when asking in what way the knowledge that is generated from users' data produces power that may be drawn on, against the interests of individuals and the majority. For Schmidt and Cohen the conflict of interest between citizens and state only exists in authoritarian states; thus they appeal to the citizens of those states to democratize their political system and to create the necessary social norms and legal regulations that will empower technological developments. According to Schmidt's and Cohen's prognosis for a kind of feel-good world, the new technologies will clearly prove useful since they allow, for example, shopkeepers in Addis Ababa or San Salvador to publicize and document state corruption and irregularities: "In fact, technology will empower people to police the police in a plethora of creative ways never before possible."[4]

This sounds very much like "digital orientalism," to borrow Evgeny Morozov's term for the self-serving Western notion that in politically "backward" countries advances in democratization are only possible with the help of Western technologies.[5] However, Schmidt and Cohen are careful not to overstate their technocentrism since it would not be in the interest of a technology corporation to concede too much power to its own products. In order to be freed from responsibility, the corporation has to delegate this power to the user. Schmidt and Cohen know better than the "do-gooder" Mark Zuckerberg that such modesty is a part of the business, and thus they dismiss proactively any possible complaints about the undesirable consequences of existing technologies with a vague appeal to civil society: "The central truth of the technology industry—that technology is neutral but people are not—will periodically be lost amid all the noise. But our collective progress as citizens in the digital age will hinge on our not forgetting it."[6]

Schmidt and Cohen are not the only ones to underline the belief that the revolution described here has only just begun and is barely understood. This is not a disquieting statement; the results of historical upheavals are rarely clear at their beginnings, as the French Revolution has shown. It is also not disturbing that the present revolution is a global one since this is the characteristic of technical revolutions as compared to political ones. It is, however, potentially explosive, in that we are hardly conscious of the fact that we are witnessing a revolution. The revolution they announce is silent, as Mercedes Bunz entitled her book in 2012, *The Silent Revolution*, inspired by Michael Angelo Garvey's *The Silent Revolution: Or, the Future Effects of Steam and Electricity Upon the Condition of Mankind* (1852). It is a revolution whose "street riots"—Klout score, Summly, Hapifork, and, of course, the stock-market algorithms—attract hardly any attention beyond that of their own individual eyewitnesses but that nonetheless change the human condition step by step and day by day—in the same way that electricity and steam once silently changed the world in the nineteenth century. Bunz proclaims the true heroes of the revolution in the subtitle of her book: *How Algorithms Are Changing Knowledge, Work, Public Life, and Politics Without Making a Lot of Noise.*

The history of this noiseless revolution is documented in another German book: Miriam Meckel's *Next. Erinnerungen an eine Zukunft ohne uns* (Next: memories of a future without us, 2011), in which an algorithm reports from the perspective of the future how once upon a time it made the uncertainties of human behavior calculable and then gradually overcame human beings altogether. The book is a sort of fictionalized science supporting the narrative of the algorithm by references to media reports on certain technical innovations: the silent "street riots" of the revolution. The end of the story is reminiscent of that of the supercomputer HAL in Stanley Kubrick's *2001: A Space Odyssey* from 1968, which eventually turns against the astronauts. Meckel's text also recalls Hans Jonas's 1979 book *The Imperative of Responsibility: In Search of an Ethics for the Technological Age*, which counters the implicit utopianism of technological advancement with an "imaginative casuistics" of the worst-case scenario: "we need the threat to the image of man—and rather specific kinds of threat—to assure ourselves of his true image. . . . *We know the thing at stake only when we know that it is at stake.*"[7]

The description of the current situation by representatives of digital-media studies reveals an alarming parallel with Meckel's prophecy of doom. After the excessive promises of salvation in the 1990s, now the arguments come from a culturally pessimistic point of view: Popular Internet theorists lament the impoverishment of relationships in a society that only communicates via media, warning that the Internet does not forget, and also that a culture of multitasking no longer trains deep reading and deep thinking.[8] Criticism is no longer limited to the jargon of digital-media studies. In its anecdotal form it also appeals to the general public, with alarmist simplifications even finding their way onto TV talk shows. A case in point is the book *Digitale Demenz—Wie wir uns und unsere Kinder um den Verstand bringen* (Digital dementia—How we drive our children out of their minds, 2012) by the neuropsychologist Manfred Spitzer. Finally, newspaper reports make sure that we are informed about the "'secret' revolution taking place.

The fact that all of this nonetheless fails to inspire a broad social debate leaves very little hope for the "imperative of responsibility." As has become very clear in the context of Snowden's disclosures in the summer of 2013, there exists a double unwillingness to expose the problems: While the general public tends to lack a sense of dissatisfaction, politicians have reduced the action of government to mere reaction, and they demonstrate political will only as isolated responses to the pressure of specific incidents. Reasons for the willingness of people to cooperate with the system of surveillance and control by digital media have already been mentioned in the first chapter. The reluctance of politicians can of course be seen as helplessness, especially when faced with global technologies that do not conform to national law. But this is only half the answer.

A more penetrating reason is to be found in Morozov's answer to a survey by the weekly *Die Zeit* from August 2013, which asked: Can the Internet still be saved? Recontextualizing the question within the discourse on modernity, Morozov notes that consumerism and surveillance dominate the net because modernity itself is dominated by consumerism and surveillance, thereby proclaiming the fate of the net to be dependent on the fate of society. The perspective that the social realm determines media might initially appear more optimistic than its counterpart, which we could term technological determinism. However, what alternatives can be offered to the free-market economy after the end of the social utopias and their discrediting in Eastern Europe, Cuba, and China? What new prospect can follow the "end of history" declared by Francis Fukuyama in 1989 after the liberal market economy and consumer society appeared as the goal of social and cultural evolution?

If Morozov's equation and Fukuyama's maxim are true, then mining big data in support of better marketing and better customer service becomes an indispensable aspect of our society. The imperative of efficiency—as the chief principle of capitalist development—has shifted from the productivity of work to the productivity of consumption. This manifests itself in the customization of offers and the classification of consumers in order to address them selectively and to exclude unprofitable transactions more effectively. To expect a sustained intervention into such practices by politicians would mean—and this is what Morozov fails to understand—committing the state to a social-utopian role in terms of educational policy. Instead of paving the way for economic growth, the state would have to begin criticizing market-inspired consumer culture as being on the wrong track, replacing it with "higher aims"—exactly the opposite of what can be expected under the conditions of neoliberalism, after the end of the social utopias. And, as we shall see, perhaps this political engagement should not be wished for at all.

Taking Morozov's statement one step further, big data is neither a sociopolitical nor a simple technological problem but a historical and philosophical one. This does not make the situation more hopeful, however. It seems that the silent technological revolution can only be halted by a loud social revolution; whether this is possible or desirable has to be discussed elsewhere. For now it must suffice to point out and note the social context of the technological revolution. The relative indifference of both politicians and the general public regarding the excesses of big-data mining can only be explained superficially by the tendency to ignore potential negative consequences in the face of instant gratification. At the same time, this indifference follows a fatalist logic stating that what can be done will be done. What is technically possible leaves no social alternative: We *scan because we can*. Even though in the time of the surveillance state a new ethics and a "new deal on data" for laws regarding individual ownership and control of one's own data are indispensable,[9] these only address one part of the problem. We will have to look at the cultural and political implications of the technological revolution by turning to its invisible heroes.

9

ALGORITHMS

At the heart and soul of all software are algorithms, the fundamental components, composed of simple instruction, of the computer world: If A then B. The "if-then" chain can be complex and may even be able to produce new "ifs" from "thens" in several consecutive steps. But we are always dealing with a finite number of steps that result, finally, in a certain output of information from a certain input. Algorithms are as old as arithmetic and geometry; Euclid's procedure for the calculation of the greatest common divisor of two numbers is nothing but the processing of certain if-then relationships in order to solve a mathematical problem. However, the golden era for algorithms arrived with the computer and the Internet, that is, once a machine based on if-then compositions could be fed with significant and now vast amounts of data. Everyone is familiar with Amazon's recommendations based on the statistical analysis of existing sales: If you are interested in such and such a book, then it is very likely you will also be interested in their recommendation. This if-then constellation—which I am invoking here as composed from socially determinative formulas, over and above the procedural if-then clauses of programming languages—is Pandora's gift from the silent revolution.

From the perspective of cultural theory, the term algorithm is of course understood in a more general way than it is in the computer sciences, whose representatives might object that even within the field's discourse the term is ambiguous.[1] On the other hand, it is precisely this distancing from the discourse of computer science as well as the metaphorical honing of the term that allows for the current gathering of different themes and debates and the development of a more generative and critical view of media technology's effects on culture. In this context I would like to note three distinct points:

1. Algorithms serve as tools to which one can turn for the solution of certain problems, adjusting them, if necessary, to concrete purposes. They are "logic plus control," as the famous 1979 dictum of the computer scientist Robert Kowalski put it.

2. With regard to computers, algorithms are not only instructions guiding technological processes (rather than human behavior, as in Euclid's case); they are always also the implementation of such instructions outside human control or regulation.

3. Algorithms interact in combination with other algorithms in complex systems and can increasingly operate according to their own directives: "Algorithms act, but they do so as part of an ill-defined network of actions upon actions, part of a complex of power-knowledge relations, in which unintended consequences, like the side effects of a program's behavior, can become critically important."[2]

This means that even though, in principle, algorithms are mathematical manifestations of cultural insight (for Amazon an insight into "similar tastes"), on a theoretical level, they develop a life of their own through their complex interactions, so that their output no longer necessarily represents a cultural input. The questionable social effect of algorithms lies in these automatic forms of data evaluation. They cannot be understood solely and instrumentally as procedures for solving problems; rather, from the perspective of social philosophy they are also the source of new problems.

But apart from the problem of algorithms' unwanted consequences, their evaluation remains ambivalent, depending on social perspective. A famous example is the anecdote at the beginning of Eli Pariser's book *The Filter Bubble: How the New Personalized Web Is Changing What We Read and How We Think* (2011), which tells us that Pariser does not receive current-events updates from his conservative friends on Facebook because Facebook's news-feed algorithm EdgeRank recognizes that he is more interested in those updates from his left-wing friends. The logic of the algorithm (which is a statistical one) thus overwrites Pariser's decision (which is an ideological one) to keep tabs on the opinions of the other side. In a world of advertisements and recommendations by Amazon, Netflix, Last.fm, and online dating sites, it may well be a welcome phenomenon that Facebook and other portals on the net are striv-ing toward personalized information design on the basis of statisti-cally calculated self-interest. But when search engines like Google present different results for the same word depending on the recent search and online activities of the user, things become problematic. If the consumer wants to be a *zoon politikon* but the filter bubble operates as an information cocoon, shielding the consumer from contradictions, it is just as bad for the individual as books that no longer spark controversy.

Those who consider the confrontation of different points of view the elixir of democracy will not regard the Internet as the prom-ised land of democratic communication but as the cozy home of an "autopropaganda"[3] that permanently validates the individual and incessantly excludes all she or he is not (yet). Personalization algo-rithms suppress chance and encounters with the Other and thus can be said to generate a kind of information-specific xenophobia of which, for the most part, one is not even aware. Hence—with respect to the social—modernity's impulse to measure turns away from the wish to know "whatever binds the world's innermost core together" and into a tool for narcissism. It is high time to reread Berthold Brecht's *Keuner* story on "Meeting Again": "A man who had not seen Mr. K for a long time greeted him with the words: 'You haven't changed a bit.' 'Oh!' said Mr. K and turned pale."[4]

This judgment concerning the filter bubble is not undisputed. After all, it is the Internet that offers space for the most contra-dictory views as well as the means for finding these perspectives through links and search engines. But if political blogs link to similarly opinionated websites 90 percent of the time,[5] one has to ask: To what extent is the possibility of escaping the bubble ever really taken advantage of? What if the real problem is not the algorithm, which, after all, could be counteracted by human intelligence? What if the problem is people themselves? This concept of a far more existential "enemy" motivated discussion on the filter bubble long before Pariser made the term popular and turned it against the algorithm. Around the turn of the millennium, Internet theoreticians assumed that humanity was an obstacle to itself insofar as it excluded all that it did not want to hear or read. One saw in digital media the possibility for people to control the information confronting them more effectively than was possible under classical mass-media newspaper and television. Although from a philosophical and political perspective this increased control is cause for concern, from a psychological perspective it fulfills the human desire for cognitive consistency. Thus the filter bubble merely automates and stabilizes, through the algorithm, something that is a human impulse. In the last analysis, it is not a technological problem but an anthropological one.[6]

Personalized recommendations and the filter bubble illustrate the deployment of the algorithms as tools for information management. The effect of this kind of information management on society is controversial because its motivation is controversial. There is also controversy as to whether the algorithm should be used as a tool for the production of information such that, with a contrary impetus, instead of being controlled by human beings, it becomes their controller.

Every platform for intercommunication on the net becomes a technology of surveillance and control through algorithmic analysis. Linguistic analysis of the data collected by Twitter and then given over to third parties provides access to social behavior, political mood, and thematic interests. This is useful as a barometer or early-warning signal not only in journalism and finance but also in healthcare, business management, and public policy. With the webcam observing us as we surf websites, every eye movement will become a contribution to statistics, and with Google Glass (or Microsoft's HoloLens, or whatever technology succeeds), it will not only be glances at the monitor but every glance that count and are counted. The algorithm turns Web 2.0—whose predecessor was regarded as anarchic—into a network for access and control. It radicalizes sociology's inner conflict: the measurement of social processes also always enables and optimizes their manipulation.

Within the context of digitization and datafication in sociology—which continues in its ambition to be an empirical, quantitative, "hard" science at least since the theoretical impetus of Gabriel Tarde (1843–1904)—a new movement was announced: computational social science.[7] This branch of social science grounds its understanding of social processes on new ways of recording data such as the "sociometer" (which compares the physical proximity of colleagues with their efficiency in communicating)[8] and on the analysis of large amounts of data from social-network profiles to patterns of movement. By being able to make credible statements concerning different if-then constellations, the question of intervention (in order to eliminate the if-basis from unwelcome then-effects) becomes more central. Interventions may certainly occur, even in the interest of the individual, when, for example, certain substances or occupations are recognized as health hazards. However, because of dwindling social-services funds and the increased aging of society, interventions are likely to be justified more often in the "interest of society as a whole." Already today accident reports and traffic tickets lead to higher insurance premiums for speeding drivers. Higher rates, however, can be prevented with the help of a "black box" in the car that sends data about driving habits to the servers of the insurance company (thereby of course also making possible the tracking of movements). In this same way, people who have unhealthy eating habits, who don't move much, or who are abusing drugs may be called to account. A foretaste of future debates took place in the discussion following the attempt of former New York City mayor Michael Bloomberg to ban supersized soft-drink bottles in 2012. While the opponents of such paternalism referred to John Stuart Mill's essay *On Liberty* (1859), according to which the individual knows best what is good for him or her, advocates of the policy were pointing out the "present-bias" problem (that is, the lack of foresight) as a justification for governmental intervention in the interest of the individual and of society.[9]

This juridical-political discussion may be the unwelcome but inevitable consequence and future of data love. Recognized correlations confront society with the question as to whether it can accept dangerous or unwanted effects knowingly or whether it is obliged to intervene. The consequence is an inversely proportional relationship between collective knowledge and individual freedom. Individual freedom is based on social ignorance—or on the socially accepted refusal to apply knowledge that has been retrieved. While algorithms bring forth more and more knowledge in the context of big-data mining, the dark side of this illumination is rarely discussed or problematized. The question of which preventive measures are justified from a social perspective must be addressed, particularly when, in the wake of the currently much-discussed predictive analytics (as a sort of statistical update of the science fiction of *Minority Report*), recognizable patterns lead to the profiling of perpetrators and to actions against "potential criminals." To a certain extent, society is held captive by the data scientists, whose discoveries can no more be reversed than those established as natural laws. Knowledge not only empowers; it also creates responsibilities. This is something we know, and not only since the publication of Friedrich Dürrenmatt's 1961 tragicomedy *The Physicians*.

However, the problematic nature of the algorithm exceeds its actual consequences. Aside from the question of how to deal with the retrieved knowledge, danger lies in the fact that social processes are increasingly defined by the algorithm's logic of if-then. If reason is reduced to formal logic, then any discussion becomes unnecessary because if-then relations do not leave any room for the "but" or the "nevertheless," nor for ambivalence, irony, or skepticism; algorithms are indifferent to context, delegating decisions to predetermined principles. As soon as algorithms operate on the basis of so-called decision-tree learning, developing classifications that are no longer defined by the programmer, the process will soon elude an understanding that is expressible in human language. The prospect of algorithmic analyses and then, based on these analyses, algorithmic regulations whose parameters cannot be understood but whose results are nevertheless binding brings to mind Kafka's scenarios of alienation more than Orwell's dystopia of surveillance. The technocratic rationality of these procedures undermines the openness of thought and thus also eradicates two of its basic virtues: the potentiality for misunderstanding and for seduction. If one clears away the gaps and strategic ambivalences from communication, thinking becomes calculation, and all that remains are determinative decisions—or simply mistakes in the combinatorial calculations.

From the point of view of the humanities-oriented sociology that Adorno opposes to an empirical-positivistic sociology, the algorithm is not an object of love but of enmity. It reduces the social to mathematics and blocks divergent, alternative positions.[10] The desire for control that underlies the concept of an algorithmic, cybernetic society is reminiscent of Ernst Bloch's utopias of order that—in contrast to the utopias of liberty and of course always in the interest of the society as a whole—aim at the efficient regulation of social life. Such desire also recalls the attempts to realize order in former socialist countries, which attempted to prevent unwelcome then-results by early intervention, suppression, and censorship at the if level. To be sure, it would be unjustified, historically, to consider the ascendancy of the algorithmic regime as Stalin's belated revenge. However, one wonders how and under what circumstances the algorithmic analysis and regulation of social behavior will, eventually, prove to be different from socialist state paternalism.

Until we can answer this question we may consider another historical analogy. The algorithm is the "Robespierre of the twenty-first century." As it was to the most famous hero of the most famous political revolution, to the hero of the present technological revolution anything human is alien; both are determined to follow a categorical idea and principle, leaving no room for misunderstandings and negotiations. The Robespierre-like steadfastness of the algorithmic is illustrated in Morozov's book *The Net Delusion*, which compares the Stasi officer in Florian Henckel von Donnersmarck's film *The Lives of Others* to an algorithm. Not only does the algorithm accomplish the same orders of surveillance more effectively than the officer; it is also reliably immune to the human. In the film, the unethical interests of the officer's superior (who desires the wife of the supposed dissident) and the musical tastes of the victim being surveilled eventually move the officer to side with his victim. Algorithms that understand music only as data to be analyzed and that do not question the moral constitution of their creators never judge their own undertaking. Their operations are not subject to any theories of good and right that might be discredited. Algorithms are the final destination of an "adiaphorized" society. They free human activity from moral concerns by letting machines take over action.[11]

Reducing rationality to calculation and logic is not simply a theoretical problem. With the Internet of things—when the floor talks to the lighting system and the swimming pool to the calendar—many situations requiring a decision will soon be (and already are) regulated by predetermined instructions: If barbecue, then heat up pool; if weight on tiles, then lights on. The Internet platforms ifttt.com and Zapier.com invite users to produce and share "Personal Recipes" for if-then processes: "Mail me if it rains tomorrow," "When you are tagged on Facebook the photo will be downloaded to Google Drive," "If a reminder is completed, append a note in Evernote."[12] At first this can be understood as a sort of man-computer symbiosis, as the computer scientist J. C. R. Licklider had foreseen in 1960: A person sets tasks and aims, and the computer carries out the routine work. However, eventually the Internet of things will also take over the process of evaluating and making decisions or, rather, have people other than the individual—the software developers, entrepreneurs, and the nerd next door—configure the different if-then relationships. The technology magazine *Wired* already sees a market for apps: "Users and developers can share their simple if-then apps and, in the case of more complex relationships, make money off of apps."[13] One no longer sells or buys objects or information but models of information processing that will inevitably disregard specific contexts.

The standardization taking place with smart things naturally develops according to the instructions of programmers. Even if users can adjust the if-then mechanism, there is always a default setting. Hackers may be able to manipulate this if-then automatism; however, the chief, essential manipulation occurs when decisions are outsourced on the grounds that one no longer has to reflect on, or be responsible for, the appropriateness of a certain reaction to a particular situation. Delegating responsibility may lie outside any moral significance when we are dealing with an automatic lighting system that by now has become standard in almost every car and many public buildings. However, this delegation becomes questionable when software programs react automatically to our environment or when the maps app on our iPhone, for example, shows street names in Bangkok in Thai script. The outsourcing of decision becomes highly charged when, with the increasing complexity of cybernetic feedback loops, it is less and less possible to comprehend on what grounds of what data the if-then loops are generated and with what consequences. It is the apotheosis of "adiaphorization" when people do not feel responsible for the effects of their actions, even when these effects and actions concern them individually.

10

ABSENCE OF THEORY

THE counterpart to the nondiscussion of the if-then model is the suppression of the theoretical by the factual. In mid-2008, *Wired*'s editor-in-chief, Chris Anderson, published an article called "The End of Theory: The Data Deluge Makes the Scientific Method Obsolete," which highlighted this idea in a provocative if simplistic way. According to Anderson, the change of method from deduction to computation accompanying the reign of the algorithm also leads to a shift in accentuation from causal relations to correlations:

> This is a world where massive amounts of data and applied mathematics replace every other tool that might be brought to bear. Out with every theory of human behavior, from linguistics to sociology. Forget taxonomy, ontology, and psychology. Who knows why people do what they do? The point is they do it, and we can track and measure it with unprecedented fidelity. With enough data, the numbers speak for themselves.[1]

Anderson's thesis encountered forceful objections: The reliability and representative efficacy of the data should be determined, the very gathering of data and their evaluation were already directed by theoretical presumptions, and merely explaining a constellation gave it epistemological weight. The first and the second objections are without doubt legitimate. The title of Lisa Gitelman's collection of essays from 2013 states this clearly: *"Raw Data" Is an Oxymoron.* Commenting on this with a media-theoretical analogy, one could argue that statistics and correlations are as "objective" as, for instance, a photograph. A photograph inevitably contains cultural determinations before and after the moment of its mechanical production—the choice of camera, the quality of the film, the object chosen to be photographed, and the context of presentation. However, as in automatic photography (Google Street View, for example), the question must be asked anew as soon as it is the algorithm itself that collects the data. The third objection questions the heuristic value of simple correlations, arguing that chance may play a role; a typical example points out the "relationship" between stork populations and birth rates. However, in contrast to such *weak* correlations, in which the growth of the first value does not lead to the growth of the second one, big data allows for the detection of *strong* correlations—correlations that may be unexplainable but, given the amount of data examined, nonetheless indisputable. If an analysis were to find a correlation between a worldwide rise of the number of storks and a higher birth rate—while considering surface area and population density—one would not on that account give the same explanation that a three-year-old might expect, but one would probably search for a third factor that could explain the findings.

That there are methodical defects in the acquisition and processing of data should not be a reason to overlook the fact that an "epistemological revolution," a transition "from research based on hypotheses to one based on data" is indeed taking place, as the philosopher of science Hans Jörg Rheinberger had already stated one year before Anderson's essay.[2] Younger scholars today are speaking with equanimity of a "post-theoretical age" in which the collecting and sorting of data pushes the generation of theses into the background; others trumpet enthusiastically that one should "forget meaning" and "follow the data stream."[3] Those who are observing the transition of the humanities into the digital humanities realize that in the meantime much of the research in the realm of literary, film, and cultural studies has been done quantitatively and that the results are neither embedded in a sound discussion of method nor in a convincing—or even interesting—theory. We should wait and see whether this situation will change with the so-called third wave of digital humanities, which will, after digitizing analogue texts and analyzing "born-digital" data, go on to reflect on the epistemic consequences of quantifying methods.[4] The institutional and financial framing of these analyses (which are aimed at mining large amounts of data quickly) and the customary form of presentation (the seductive aesthetics of interactive visualizations) appear very unlikely to be conducive to the lengthy process of forming theses in any case.

Ultimately, the important question will be whether the organization of data will eclipse the formation of theories temporarily or whether the specifics of the "what" in the end will make the "why" question obsolete. While in the economic system (whose currency, according to Niklas Luhmann, is not truth but money) the "why" only plays a secondary role as long as the "what" proves practical, in the system of the sciences, traditionally, the desire to understand counts for more than practicality. On the one hand, it would contradict human nature not to ask *why* something is the way it is. On the other hand, more and more often *pure* science gives way to an applied science that targets solutions over truths. Moreover, the "why" question is already regarded as a possible drawback, depicted as the hypotheses-based obscuration of possible solutions: "Insights are distorted again as soon as causality is brought back into the game."[5] This thought becomes radicalized by translating the "post-theoretical age" into a post*ideological* one: "In the absence of data, you theorise. In an abundance, you just need to do the maths. And, because of all those super-efficient search engines, we share more and more data. Data dissolves ideology."[6] This kind of cheerful abstinence from theory finally makes us ask whether we are able to imagine a culture in which the "that" (something is like this) makes the "why" (therefore it is like this) superfluous, especially when the latter is no longer at the center of education.

This question becomes especially urgent in an expanded frame of reference. One cannot overlook the fact that big-data mining changes our relationship to the world and to knowledge. Outside the history of technology, similar but less-known movements have been taking place in historiography and aesthetic theory since the 1980s. When, for instance, the French historian Pierre Nora speaks of the "conquest and eradication of memory by history," he also points out the replacement of historical narratives—or theories, for that matter—by the archive filled with "raw data."[7] In aesthetic theory, the aesthetics of the sublime, of performance, and of presence—dissimilar regarding their terminology, methods, and aims—intersect and concur in their focus on materiality and intensity of experience at the expense of meaning and interpretation.[8] It is symptomatic of these circumstances when Jean-François Lyotard consigns contemporary art to the rhetoric of a pure presence of color and form: "When we have been abandoned by meaning, the artist has a professional duty to bear witness that *there* is, to respond to the order to be. The painting becomes evidence, and it is fitting that it should not offer anything that has to be deciphered, still less interpreted."[9] Also symptomatic is Hans Ulrich Gumbrecht's appeal for a movement away from "meaning cultures," with hermeneutics and interpretation as core components of the humanities, to "presence cultures" that aim at intensity and unmediated proximity to the things of the world.[10]

The analogy between the epistemological model of correlation and the aesthetic one of the sublime may be surprising given the contradictoriness of abstract signs and quantifying expressions. After all, in big-data mining we are dealing with "predictive analysis" in contradistinction to the aesthetics of the sublime, which is related to the moment. In mining big data the spirit does not feel disempowered by the appearance of the unfathomable, as is the case with the sublime, but rather empowered by reliable knowledge. The common ground between the model of correlation and the aesthetics of the sublime, however, lies in a shared abstinence with respect to theory. The sublime of big-data mining can be seen in the fact that the object is not interpreted but simply perceived. The form of knowledge of the "that" without the "why" mirrors the model of perception of the "that" instead of the "what." Decisive here is the different effect of the renewed turn against interpretation in big-data mining: The sublime of big data eludes both the epistemological crisis, to which the aesthetics of the sublime was a reaction, and the return to the strong epistemologies that preceded it.

Lyotard's concept of the aesthetics of the sublime was a logical consequence of his theory of postmodernism. The sublime—the shock one cannot come to terms with—is an answer to Lyotard's declaration of the end of the grand narratives that—under the banner of humanism, Christianity, or socialism—provided history with a telos and legitimized human action. Therefore, Jacques Rancière later regards the "disaster" of the sublime" (disaster because it bears witness to the insurmountable alienation of postmodern man) as a protection from the "disaster of the promise of emancipation" that wakes us "from a sleep-filled life of consumption, only to throw us headlong into the fatal utopias of totalitarianism."[11] The correlation of interpretation and ideology implied here hones the question at hand: Does the end of theory (loudly proclaimed by Anderson in the face of the big-data paradigm, easily welcomed by Brian Eno as the end of ideology, and in the meantime propagated or simply practiced by younger scholars) mean the rescue from fatal utopias, as Rancière calls it, or from new narratives of legitimation, as Lyotard would have had it?

Against this background, data love is not only an emotional reaction to the technological development of the early twenty-first century but also a political answer to the philosophical problem of postmodernism at the end of the twentieth century. This reaction had been predicted at the end of the 1990s when Norbert Bolz, using the keyword *theory fatigue*, announced that the new, posthistorical world stabilizes in factual knowledge.[12] Granted, these concerns were already there at the beginning of the 1980s when Lyotard warned about the "victory of capitalist technoscience over the other candidates for the universal finality of human history" through "increased reliance on facts," a reliance that would accept only success as a criterion of judgment though "incapable of saying what success is, or why it is good, just, or true." For Lyotard, mastering objects by way of their factuality "does not complete the project of realizing universality but in fact accelerates the process of delegitimation."[13] But what would be its realization? The disaster of the sublime? A new fatal utopia? Taken positively: The quantitative turn of big-data mining offers a utopia and a narrative of legitimation in the "if-then" mode without generating new theories. The end of the great narratives shifts the business of teleology from mythical predictions, the philosophy of history's designs, and "historical regularities" to correlations that inform future actions without the burden of having to explain them retrospectively. The "joy of the number" beyond narration?

PART III

THE JOY OF NUMBERS

11

COMPULSIVE MEASURING

A HILL whose height remained unknown was an insult to the intelligence, muses Alexander von Humboldt in Daniel Kehlmann's novel *Measuring the World* (2007). There were many surveyors in the nineteenth century—and not only during this period. Cartography was a part of the movement to measure the world, as was Linné's botanical taxonomy of the species or Franz-Josef Gall's phrenological work, promising—based on the physiognomy of Johann Kaspar Lavater—to be able to infer the characteristics of a person from the dimensions and form of his or her skull. And then there was the prospect of a glimpse inside the skull, into the depths of the unconscious, thanks to Sigmund Freud's dream-work and psychoanalysis. To measure, to count, to weigh, to unearth, and to uncover was the stimulus of modernity, and rationality was its guide.

No wonder that once rationality was radicalized as formal logic through computation this would lead to excesses of measurement—especially given the fact that nowadays surveyors no longer need to risk their lives as von Humboldt had. Decoding the human genome and making neuroscientific analyses take place within the safe confines of the workplace or lab, as does the deciphering of human behavior, which is made possible because networked computers not only create a huge capacity for computation but also subject the social realm to the blanket collection of data. Visits to websites, searches, the purchase of tickets, transcriptions of verbal exchanges—nothing that happens online escapes the attention of algorithms. Thanks to smart phones, GPS, and RIFD, what happens in RL—"real life," in contradistinction to the virtual life of cyberspace—is mirrored on the Internet as well.

Facebook's Gross National Happiness Index illustrates the excess and absurdity of big-data mining by counting the use of positive and negative words in Facebook's status updates. Another example is Hedonometer.org, which scours Twitter, *New York Times* articles, Google Books, and music lyrics for keywords. The knowledge derived from Facebook's research is that people are generally happier around Christmas and that Catalonians are also happier on Sant Jordi and Americans on Super Bowl Sunday.[1] The insights from Hedonometer are more interesting since it also analyzes the places from which the tweets are sent. Thus it discovers that people feel altogether happier if they are not at home, which, on the one hand, is surprising and, on the other, may not be—depending on one's perspective on life. The interpretation of data, however, is not only relative to human perspectives. The danger of obvious misunderstandings is ever present when the analysis is undertaken by artificial intelligence. This kind of thing delights the investment company Berkshire Hathaway, which is happy every time the actress Anne Hathaway appears in a new film because the value of its shares rises—and even more so the more scantily she is dressed. The shares do not rise in value because the actress owns the company but because trading algorithms assume that the more often the name Hathaway appears, the more people will be interested in the investment company.[2]

But matters are more serious than these examples might suggest. In the first place, there is a lot of money to be made with data. Empirical studies confirm a connection between Facebook's happiness score and stock-market values. Anyone who does a thorough analysis of communications regarding financial markets in social media will understand the "psychology of the stock market" and may even be able to make predictions about its future development.[3] This creates high expectations—and leads to many new startups. What is *the* subject of the moment on Twitter? No problem. Who sends the most tweets and receives the most retweets? No problem. Which video is the hottest, which piece of music, which politician, which country, which website, which search, which electronic book, which passage in that book?—no problem at all! The data traces we create become the shadow of our online existences—and a paradise for statisticians, sociologists, corporations, and intelligence agencies.

This shadow can only be shed by those who act like the hero in the German writer Adelbert von Chamisso's *Peter Schlemihl* (1814)—namely, by getting involved with the underworld: by doing whatever is necessary to become anonymous, traveling the net more or less incognito. Nevertheless, valuable data can still be gathered since information on how long somebody lingers somewhere allows for the compilation of behavioral patterns and indices of normalcy even if this somebody remains anonymous. Admittedly, the statistical analysis becomes more concrete as soon as the identity of the user is known. However, following analysis, the pressure to optimize—on, for example, the editorial team of an online journal or with respect to any web offer—operates just as effectively with numbers that are indisputable even if derived from anonymous sources.

To make processing easier, measurement-friendly forms of communication such as views, likes, and shares were created, allowing for a translation of the opinions generated by Web 2.0 use into measurable currency. The binary operational mode of digital media—zero/one, yes/no—thus becomes effective beyond the interface. From this point of view, the medium's message is that society is constructed of dichotomies, and, to a certain extent, it is also infantilized, dissolving complex matters into the nuance-free, fairy-tale alternatives of good or bad. At one and the same time this dichotomizing is a sophisticated strategic move attempting to solve the problems of interpretation at the point of entry. Instead of laborious, ambivalent—let alone ironic—commentary, we get unequivocal, measurable votes.

This is exactly what makes statistics so attractive. They appear factual, subject to economics, mercilessly neutral, and can be universally understood, even by observers outside the discipline. Communication in terms of numbers generates trust efficiently and is construable for those who remain clueless. On the basis of numbers, even managers without any critical or cinema background can make judgments about what films should be shown and which should be taken out of the schedule. Quantification allows for decision making without having to make a decision. This is the end of cultural rule by experts—not through an opening up of discourse to everyone but merely by switching from word to number. The statistical view of society establishes a numeratocracy.[4]

The evocation of Chamisso's *Schlemihl* is more important than previously intimated. He bargained with the devil and traded his shadow for a purse permanently filled with gold, but he was, thereby, excluded from his bourgeois background. He who has no shadow has no identity. And it is this that holds the future danger currently being discussed under the rubric "I post, therefore I am": Those who do not create a data trace do not exist. This is already true of social networks, within which service providers are pushing anyone who resists the constant requirement for transparency to the margins of social communication. As everyone knows, data traces are indispensable in other areas. Without a credit history there is no credit; without a history of incidents there is no insurance protection. One cannot assume that more effective technologies of identification will decrease the demand that human subjects should identify themselves.

Data acquisition will increasingly become a social duty and will be perceived as being in the interest of the public good to the extent that one will not be able to avoid the provision of personal data without consequences. Public access to all medical records, for example, is not only desired by interested parties on Internet portals such as PatientsLikeMe.com, whose visitors are greeted with this tagline: "Making healthcare better for everyone through sharing, support, and research." The rhetoric of sharing implicitly labels those who withhold their data as egoistic and asocial. In the era of big data, concern for our fellow men no longer shows itself in the sharing of one's coat but in the sharing of one's data. "Sharing is caring" reads the slogan at Circle, a combination of Google and Facebook in Dave Eggers's dystopia *The Circle* (2014)—with the inevitable flipside: "privacy is theft." To participate in society, we must have a data shadow. Those who withhold it will one day find themselves cut off from medical care, just like Violet, the rebellious woman in M. T. Anderson's dystopian science-fiction novel *Feed* (2002).

12

THE PHENOMENOLOGY
OF THE NUMERABLE

HOW society will deal with individual data traces in the future remains to be seen and in the best-case scenario will depend on a commensurate public discussion. Let us first consider how the quantitative approach looks today.

Aesthetically, statistics promote spectacle by creating numerical comparability: vertically, concerning the development of a measured object (sales numbers for a business, votes for a party, popularity of a show or a university), and horizontally, when the results are correlated with competitors. Visual presentation creates dramatic effects: the growing bar, the precipitous curve, complex animations between the X- and Y-axis generating suspense and entertainment on a par with sports events—there is always a winner when there is a ranking. One could also call this "gamification"—the transfer of game logic onto the rest of life. At the same time, ranking creates a simple, childlike worldview within which one still has a favorite color, food, doll, or friend and is still asking questions like "Who do you love more, dad or me?"

The Internet extends competition to every YouTube video, every weblog, and every newspaper article by way of countable views, likes, and comments. It encompasses the individual through numbers of friends on Facebook, likes on Instagram, retweets on Twitter. The comparison of numbers becomes a popular sport, but because sport has losers, these networks do not only signify fun; they also breed frustration and envy, in light of the great results that so many others have obtained.[1]

Statistics conquers all-new realms by way of the Quantified Self movement, whose motto, "Living by Numbers," does not actually turn people into numbers; rather, it creates identities from numbers and celebrates winners who have the best figures or who, in the end, reach the most advanced age. Self-trackers are baited by products geared toward personal-fitness programs. The names "Fitbit" and "Digfit" already point to this. Naturally, in the era of Web 2.0, sharing is endemic within the world of tracking, and thus trackers will expose their data on networks like DailyMile.com or runtastic.com in order to make comparisons with others. On gym-pact.com—where users pledge to pay a penalty to the more disciplined members if they skip their scheduled training—one can even capitalize on sharing. "Social running" makes use of the Hawthorne effect—known from ergonomics—under the influence of which one works more when one is being observed. Transparency becomes an aid to motivation.[2] With smart things, like the Hapifork, entering into everyday life, unimagined possibilities for applications present themselves. If the prospects pan out, then all of us will be one another's permanent audience, constantly competing for self-optimization—with doctors and insurance agents as our referees in the cloud. If employers are also becoming interested in measuring bracelets when they are fastened to the wrists of their employees, this will not spoil the fun.[3]

Statistics are the advocates of the grassroots. They radicalize democracy into numeratocracy by subtraction. Statistics remove any need for the articulation of opinion and replace it with an act of silent voting. The comment function in online contributions still somewhat distorts this move from words to numbers by allowing people to procure advantage for themselves through rhetorical proficiency. It is only the enumeration of views, shares, and likes that guarantees an equal right to be heard regardless of all differences in education or financial prosperity.

With a democracy based on binary dichotomies Jean-Jacques Rousseau wins out against Nicolas de Condorcet, who had preferred representative democracy over direct democracy, given the masses' lack of enlightenment and competence. Although Condorcet qualified his views by way of his own jury theorem, according to which the relative probability of a correct answer to a yes-or-no question increases with the size of the group being polled, in the end he preferred representative democracy because it gives power to those who discover what they are talking about after reflection and discussion, thereby securing the rule of expertise over numbers. For Rousseau, on the other hand, in a true democracy talking is silver and counting is gold. As he suggests in his *Social Contract*, the general will can be best recognized when citizens don't communicate with one another at all. Rousseau maintained that communication meant illustrating differences in order to eliminate them through the soft coercion of the better argument, as Jürgen Habermas later suggested in his discourse ethics of the ideal speech situation. But such a condition only exists theoretically. In practice, the elimination of difference occurs as capitulation to better rhetoric, social position, power of promises, and power over media. For Rousseau, communication is manipulation, and it distorts the individual's original point of view.

In this light, the numerical-mathematical rationality is superior to the communicative-discursive variety. Statistics recognize a general will of everyone on all possible subjects more truly than any representative democracy. If nothing else, this is important in an era of hyphenated identities where hardly anyone still finds his or her political views represented in one single political party. A statistical approach privileges issues over predetermination, for example, voting on a case-by-case basis rather than for a prepackaged political program. If every piece of information is taken into consideration for every single case, big-data mining is a shift from synthetic-discursive exclusion to syndetic-additive inclusion.[4]

A good example of direct-democratic radicalization under the banner of the number—and for the problematic consequences of quantification—is silent voting in online publications. When every article in a paper can be called up individually, such pieces as the sophisticated opinion column or complex cultural essay lose their blanket protection, something they enjoyed in the overall design package of the printed edition. In print, the "high-brow" column rises above the relatively "lightweight" contributions on earthquakes, plane crashes, political scandals, celebrity divorces, or everyman's family dramas, even though these attract the bulk of the readership. By contrast, the individualized counting of online views discloses the true interests of reader-customers and exposes concealed subsidies.[5] The keyword for democracy for Web 2.0 is "social bookmarking." Statistics, as the incorruptible seismograph of society, become the tireless advocate of the majority.

Statistics increase control because they create mean values and behavioral patterns allowing for the detection of divergences or similarities. The target of this control is, in part, prognosis and prevention. A company with the telling name Recorded Future predicts events and trends—regardless of whether they are elections or protests— and advertises with the tagline "Unlock the Predictive Power of the Web." Part of this power is the revelation of connections between people, places, and organizations. Just as a high rate of signals from mobile phones within a constrained area makes us expect a traffic jam, a high number of retweets tied to certain telltale words may signal the emergence of a political trendsetter even before that individual perceives him- or herself to be one.

The question remains the same: Who is using this power? Of course, the answer is not only businesses and government institutions but also citizen movements and NGOs. Big-data mining can serve the most divergent interests. However, inasmuch as complex and accurate data mining has its price, the insights one can afford will depend on the scope of one's means. Inevitably, this will increase the knowledge divide between the powerful and affluent in society and those constituencies of the general public whose data are analyzed but who do not themselves have the knowledge or means to participate in such analyses. As for the analysts, one can hardly expect that they will allow their work to suffer because of ethical considerations. In their "search for truth" they will answer the questions of their customers as accurately and as efficiently as possible.

As control begins to take hold, it reveals the tools of its control since those who become aware of how data is rendered suspect will avoid producing such data. Cautious Facebook users are already censoring themselves today because they don't want to discredit themselves or their friends with potential employers. The many possibilities for data analysis will not be kept secret. They will be made visible in the name of transparency. However, such transparency will undermine precisely what characterizes true democracy: the possibility of choosing to be different. The transparent citizen may become the "unknown citizen" that the British poet W. H. Auden describes in his 1939 poem of that title. In addition to the lines transcribed as the epigraph to this book one should consider its closing lines as well: "Was he free? Was he happy? The question is absurd: / Had anything been wrong, we should certainly have heard."

The relational understanding of culture fostered by society determined by statistics is, at the same time, the end of postmodernism's legacy of relativism. Relating numbers does not make them relative to one another philosophically. Numbers offer up an epistemological happy ending that will prove popular with all those who have never reconciled themselves to ironic liberalism and cynical rationality.

It is a truism of educational theory that having more knowledge at our disposal does not necessarily provide us with more knowledge in terms of orientation. In fact, an inversely proportional relationship is implied. The increase of knowledge about hitherto unknown matters as a function of globalization (as well as multi- or transcultural transformation of the social realm) undermines orientational knowledge and also the ability to act, which had been previously fostered by the local context.[6] Added to this is the undermining of knowledge that occurs following on from the methodical application of self-reflection and skepticism. Incredulity with respect to objective knowledge undermines claims of universality. Instead there is talk of a multiplicity of language games, each with their own specific rationalities within their respective limited scopes. Those who do not close off this perspective accept other worldviews and cultural patterns as equal to their own and therefore regard their own with a grain of salt.

Insofar as knowledge entails the working out of information in cultural patterns of orientation aimed at a definite course of action, the description of the present age as a "knowledge society" is a misnomer. The term "information society" is more fitting, for this society is predicated on the increase of information and information technologies, that is, on systemic factors rather than individual experiences. It would be even more accurate to talk of a "data society" not only because of the enormous and ubiquitous accumulation, analysis, and love of data but also because data mining presents itself as the solution for the crisis in knowledge and its claims to statistical objectivity.

Thirty years ago the fear arose that science and theory had immunized themselves against far-reaching claims of clarification and validity and that this could open the door "to a feudalization of scientific knowledge practice through economic and political interests and 'new dogmas.' . . . Science, having lost reality, faces the threat that others will dictate to it what truth is supposed to be."[7] Since then society has been computerized to such an extent that the sciences—inclusive of the hermeneutical strongholds of literature and art—are practiced under the influence of algorithmic data analysis. Statistics methodically strengthened the ideal of democracy and, in the social realm, provided a certain new self-confidence to the sciences. In the beginning was the word; now the proclivity for naming yields to trust in numbers. "You can't improve or understand what you can't measure," as Hedonometer.org advertises for its happiness index.[8] This is the rhetoric of the new era: Knowledge is numerical. In the end was the number.

But even salvation is a scam. A famous example of big-data mining is Google's Flu Trend. Since 2008 this algorithm has been inferring the frequency of flu cases from the rate of related search terms much faster than national Centers for Disease Control and Prevention, which have to rely on information from doctors. But in 2013, Google's information was so inaccurate that the algorithmic procedure creating the statistics became heavily suspect. For others, this was no more than a rookie mistake that could be remedied with cautious methodical revision. In the case of Google's Flu Trend this meant identifying and removing, for example, those search queries that were not prompted by personal concern but by mere interest in a subject that had become popular in the media. The problem of statistics is the insecurity of its analytical criteria. If May 2, 2011, the day on which Osama Bin Laden was shot by a special unit of Navy Seals, was not a very "happy day" according to the Hedonometer .org, the reason is, clearly, not that most of the twitterers were Islamists mourning Bin Laden's death but rather because on this day substantially more words were used that have minimal value in Hedonometer's happiness rank: "death" (1.54 out of 9), "killed" (1.56), "terrorist" (1.30).[9] This is another example of distortion in the "results" of statistical analyses caused by inadequate interpretation of data.

Statistics cannot escape the cultural, ideological, or narrative domains. The ways in which measuring procedures are framed make them disputable—the intentions underlying queries for flu-related keywords, the ranking of words indicating happiness—and thus the data has to be queried more and more thoroughly: What is being measured, and why not a different aspect of reality? How is it being measured, and why not with other methods? Which data are being compared, and why not with other criteria? How were the reference groups created, and why not others? Decisions that pertain to quality come as much before quantification as they do later, in the process of editing. The use of linguistic and graphic elements favors certain socially acceptable ways of reading—and this often leads to sim-plifications pitched at the public's perceived ability to understand. Computer scientists therefore speak of "conceptual representation," sociologists of "qualculation."[10]

The other technical term used in the critique of statistics is "Campbell's Law." This law, coined by the sociologist Donald T. Campbell in 1976, teaches us that the method of analysis manipu-lates the object of investigation. The greater the use of quantitative social indicators for social decision making, the greater the risk that subjects will be influenced by these indicators in their actions and thus face the possibility that the indicators will distort and corrupt the social processes they are intended to monitor. An example is the statistical evaluation of scientific quality. The procedure is well known. The value of an article is measured according to the impact factor of its place of publication, which results, in turn, from its citation indices. The mistake in the evaluation of this calculation lies in the difficulty in distinguishing between "slaves" and "masters." Many articles in top publications are rarely quoted or in any case not more often than certain articles in a publication with a lesser impact factor.[11] The danger of the abuse of this procedure—Campbell's Law—lies in the opportunism of authors who design subjects, sources, and theses for a top journal by specifically targeting the preferences of its editors and likely evaluators. The statistical method of assessment may thus serve to hinder innovative perspectives that have, as yet, no lobby, and this can result in research positions not being filled by brilliant thinkers but by persons with a higher systems competence.

13

DIGITAL HUMANITIES

I F in former times it was possible that an unmeasured hill could insult rationality, it is now rationality that—statistically instrumentalized—insults itself. The excesses in measurement of the cybernetic era turn rationality—radicalized as formal logic in the computer—into its own opponent. The delight in statistics, today so emphatically embraced, entails serious side effects: the aesthetics of the spectacle, the danger of populism, an illusion of truth, and the distortion of reality. Added to this is the internalization of the statistical perspective by society, which moves from quantified evaluations to yes/no dichotomies.

What is set out here from a perspective of cultural pessimism for others holds all the promises of the future, and not only for civil servants and businessmen. Science also invests high hopes in the "computational turn," as do the humanities. The discussion is being carried out under the rubric of the "digital humanities" and aims at implementing algorithmic methods of analysis for humanities scholarship. Such methods have been practiced for some time in linguistics and computer-assisted philology in the form of automated corpus analysis, but they are now being widely adopted as a standard methodology. "The Humanities Go Google" is the title of an article on mathematizing the humanities that was featured as critique rather than promotion in *The Chronicle of Higher Education, Technology*.[1] A prime example for work of this kind is that

by the English professor Franco Moretti, the founder and director of the Literary Lab at Stanford University and author of books
such as *Graphs, Maps, Trees: Abstract Models for a Literary History*
(2005) and *Distant Reading* (2013). Distant reading—the algorithmic analysis of texts based on word occurrences and lexical patterns—is a requirement for graphs and maps. Only if a computer
reads all the available texts of an epoch—as opposed to the literary
scholar who, through close reading, covers at best only a bit more
than the canon—can statistical statements on literary processes be
turned into something that can be visualized. Moretti coquettishly
calls it "a little pact with the devil: we know how to read texts, now
let's learn how *not* to read them."[2] It is a pact with the devil because
it turns literary history away from reading and toward counting. It
makes the literary text—whether canonized or not—disappear in
macroperspectival structures.

It is exactly this paradigm of the number that more and more
programs of research within the humanities adopt. The results can
be found in several text collections with the term "digital humanities" in the title as well as in new research branches and methods like
"culturomics" and "cultural analytics" as quantitative cultural studies
of sorts. This process has been criticized as an academic variant of
the neoliberal remodeling of society and as the sellout of science to
the economic concept of efficiency.[3] One can also understand it as a
twofold answer to the problem of postmodern information society:
All data are processed *free of theory*.

The promise of the computational turn for the humanities is new
quality by way of new quantity. On the one hand, considerably more
data can be parsed through automated processes than by human
beings, and the results can be visualized in a manner substantially
more insightful than by way of texts alone. The hope is that human
insight can be saved from the information overload of current technologies precisely by the adoption of new technologies. On the
other hand, the authority of data allows science to be liberated from
subjective theories—the science that had previously dethroned
itself by the exercise of methodological skepticism against its own
methodologies. In a positivistic statistical mode—ideally as data

processing without theory—rationality looks for a way out of its self-imposed lack of credibility. Regarding the danger of the feudalization of scientific knowledge, the sciences now answer the challenge with two projects for the democratization of knowledge: the supposed transparency of numbers and the popular production and discussion of numbers through the self-tracking movement—as empirical sociology "from below."

If it is still true that our writing tools influence our thoughts—as Nietzsche once said about his typewriter—then in the context of the computational turn we cannot escape addressing the epistemological consequences of rule by algorithm. One such consequence is formalization according to the model of computational logic, a logic that inscribes itself into intellectual engagement by breaking down inquiry, analysis, and presentation into discrete entities, much in the spirit of the basic principles of digital technologies: classification, organization, navigation. An example of this practice is associated with "linked data," a concept initially introduced in 2006 by Tim Berners-Lee, the inventor of the World Wide Web. The aim is to dissect thought and information into the smallest entities, with predicates that can be interrelated. The political manifestation of this concept would be to network, in the name of "linked open data," all online databases without restrictions and in the interest of the general public. At one and the same time, "linked data" is of epistemological importance. It consistently treats statements as facts, necessarily therefore divesting them of their contextual framework and relationships. Only discrete items of data—"raw data," as it is called in the promotional video on data.europeana.eu—can be identified by algorithms and so connected in a flexible manner.

One form of the linked-data concept, the "semantic web" that conforms texts to machine-readable formats, is known as nanopublication: "A nanopublication is the smallest unit of publishable information: an assertion about anything that can be uniquely identified and attributed to its author."[4] The aim of this procedure is to accommodate texts to a schema based on RDF (Resource Description Framework), which translates every statement into a relation of two entities, that is, into the sequence subject–predicate–object.

One example of such a "tripel" is: *The nanopublication* [subject] *translates into discrete entities* [predicate] *thought* [object].[5] What sounds technical and unfamiliar for a scholar of humanities is nevertheless clear in its agenda. The formalization and classification of statements through semantic markup provides the computer with a representation of the structure and meaning of such a publication and allows for efficient and flexible search, integration, and recombination of information. The intention of this formalized representation of knowledge in nanopublication follows the principles of databases, attributing metadata frameworks to statements and entries (such as name, place, date, address, etc.) so that these can be flexibly related to one another. At nanopub.org, researchers are now also invited to implement these procedures with the implicit warning that if they do not, they risk being excluded from citation networks: "Because nanopublications can be attributed and cited, they provide incentives for researchers to make their data available in standard formats that drive data accessibility and interoperability."

This formalization of meaning was notably criticized from cultural theory's point of view, above all for the implicit presumption that an unequivocal, universally valid ontology on the basis of formal specifications could be established. Against this type of "technocratic neo-scholasticism," cultural theory points out that metadata embeds more or less subjective perspectives and that these do not express reality but rather a relationship to reality.[6] Countering this, computer scientists perceive it as a misconception and point out that the semantic web in no way enforces the determination of terms according to a singular framework and that semantic markups can also result from "social mechanisms in communities that provide large-scale human-produced markup."[7] Nevertheless, we should ask what role these social markups play when they produce a statistically deduced "winning opinion" and to what extent semantic multiplicity and plural ontologies can truly be experienced when, in practice, the ontologies remain hidden behind the user interface.[8]

As long as the semantic web is the subject of hopes and fears and has not yet become established practice, these questions have to remain open. Regardless, the antithesis of nanopublication remains a text that does not see itself as a set of isolated statements but as a process of thought. As the Latin source of the term indicates, the text is a web, and as such it is more than the sum of its parts. The originality of a text, and especially that of a monograph, lies in the "transgression of operable information units" and in the multiple connections with other discourses developed beyond any discrete core statements.[9] This openness—which at the same time stubbornly resists any reduction into separate units of argumentation—is taken to the extreme in the form of the essay, which Adorno conceived as the quasi-anarchistic corrective for methodology in the humanities. In Adorno's conception the essay— "radical in its non-radicalism, in refraining from any reduction to a principle"—enacts the "consciousness of nonidentity"; this is one of the main points of Adorno's *Negative Dialectics*.[10] The essay abstains and refrains from "the pre-critical obligation to define," recognizing "that the demand for strict definitions has long served to eliminate—through stipulative manipulations of the meanings of concepts—the irritating and dangerous aspects of the things that live in the concepts." For Adorno, this rejection is characteristic of the essay, as is its "lack of a standpoint," which resists "the notion of truth as something 'fixed,' a hierarchy of concepts."[11] Therefore the essay "proceeds methodically unmethodically"; it experiments with a train of thought that "turns his object around, questions it, feels it, tests it, reflects on it." The essay ensures that "what is contingent and isolated in its insights" is not corrected "by a process of abstraction that ends in characteristic features derived from them"; it denies being reduced to entities or even to a general statement.[12]

This culture of reasoning—foregoing both conceptual fixation and definitive statements—turns the text into an artful composition that continually emulates the aesthetic characteristics of its field of reference, above all in literary studies. Georg Lukács has therefore spoken of the "argument as a form of art" in his essay collection *Soul and Form*, stressing that in the case of the essay form supersedes content to the extent that the essay itself would still be worth reading even after its content has been refuted.

It is easy to see to what extent this perspective contradicts cognitive conceptions that rely on the precision of numbers as opposed to the ambivalence of language. The difference lies mainly in the approach to identification. While Adorno's essay remains open by deferring and avoiding identification or delimitation, the concept of linked data aims at the connection of what previously had been identified as distinct; just as in political discourse whatever is "international" is chiefly conceived in terms of antedated formations and the demarcation of nations. In the course of the computational turn in the humanities, Adorno's perspective has as few prospects as his social philosophy, which will be discussed later on.

One could object that, on the one hand, Adorno's hypothesis does not fully represent the humanities and, on the other, that—to come back to the initial example—quantifying distant reading does not have to mean the end of interpretive close reading. Rather, distant reading can furnish us with new questions that may, in their turn, be addressed with essayistic ambivalence or even in the mode of "screwing around" with hermeneutics.[13] The fact that nanopublication is being discussed, initially, as a phenomenon of the natural sciences and that the semantic web has not yet developed any practical relevance is possibly also somewhat reassuring. In the context of the digitalization of the humanities, however, the question has to be asked when the general changeover from telling to tallying will ultimately undermine the text—and the essay—as sites of insight and respected forms of publication. There had been forays in this direction as early as twenty years ago, and notably in a humanities context, when hypertext was erroneously declared the royal road of critical discourse.

A hypertext is a web of loose threads. Even though the words and links are still attributable to the author, the coherence is not. Hypertext segments the text into a multiplicity of its parts, variable and recombinant, just as nanopublication intends. In the early 1990s, a time heavily influenced by postmodern philosophy and literary theory, many literary scholars greeted the arrival of hypertext euphorically. They celebrated the structure of the flexible cross-linkages as a liberation from the tyrannies of the author and linear narrative and viewed hypertext as the practical application of postmodern theory. George P. Landow's influential book expressed this conviction in its title: *Hypertext: The Convergence of Contemporary Critical Theory and Technology* (1991). Above all, there was the belief that texts would lose their "discreteness" through the linking of their contexts.[14] That this was a misdirected conclusion was already apparent by 1994, as evidenced in the pertinent cultural-theoretical collection on hypertext entitled *Hyper/Text/Theory*. Manifold linking is preceded by atomization. This creates autonomous, context-free, textual units and does not allow for the elaboration of philosophical arguments—let alone deconstructionist maneuvers.[15]

From this perspective the technologies of hypertext are revealed not as an advocate of postmodern thought but rather as among its adversaries. The technology of hypertext no longer allows for ambivalence and destabilization internally, between the lines, but only externally, between the recombinant textual units—that is, in exactly the same way that the concepts of nanopublication and linked data propose. If, apart from its attention to the elaborated, detailed text as a classical form of discussion, the digital humanities demands training in the short form—"which distills the long and the large into compact form"[16]—then this appears also to be a step in the direction of semantic web–style publishing, namely as variable cross-linking and continuous intercommunication among isolable units as predicates. It remains to be seen to what extent the other privileged forms of presentation in digital media—visualizations, animations, interactions—can be employed not only for the sake of illustration and simplification but so as to create ambiguity and deconstruction.

14

LESSING'S REJOINDER

THE principle of nanopublication not only radicalizes hyper-textuality; it also corresponds with the idea that narration is being superseded by the database as the new reigning model "to make meaning out of the world,"[1] in the words of Lev Manovich as early as 2001. Thus, certain structures of events and information are replaced by the flexible (re)combination of data. The conceptions of the information society are different in principle from the Humboldtian educational ideal that had understood the acquisition of knowledge as a process and not as a mediation of information, and this is occasionally acknowledged in discussions of the digital humanities.[2] The new technologies, according to the prognosis, replace "the Humboldtian subject filled with culture and a certain notion of rationality" with the "computational subject" that knows "where to recall culture as and when it was needed in conjunction with computationally available others, a *just-in-time* cultural subject."[3] This "just-in-time" mode describes the situational focus of the "computational subject," whose accompanying experience is that of impermanence. "Just-in-time" means "at once" but also "only for now." The cumulative acquisition and retention of knowledge give way to a masterful juggling of knowledge: "'doing knowledge' instead of 'having knowledge.'"[4]

It is less obvious what this change in knowledge management means from the perspective of the sociology of knowledge: a change of emphasis from process to product. The situational juggling has no time for tedious processes of reception; it expects "offers" of knowledge with an exact product description for which relevant parameters are available: thesis, result, keywords, and construction of content. This procedure diametrically opposes a textual formation like that of the essay, one that invites the reader to embark on a journey whose destination remains uncertain. Why such a being-on-the-road may nevertheless be its destination will become clear if we turn to one of the most prominent representatives of the Enlightenment and a mastermind for the Humboldtian educational ideal: Gotthold Ephraim Lessing.

In 1787 Lessing wrote a small text on truth and the path to knowledge entitled *A Rejoinder* as part of his *Philosophical and Theological Writings*. He proclaims: "If God held fast in his right hand the whole of truth and in his left hand only the ever-active quest for truth, albeit with the proviso that I should constantly and eternally err, and said to me: 'Choose!', I would humbly fall upon his left hand and say: 'Father, give! For pure truth is for you alone!'"[5] The falling upon God's left hand is a decision against the product and for the process. As Lessing maintains: "Not the truth which someone possesses or believes he possesses but the honest effort he has made to get at the truth, constitutes a human being's worth. For it is not through the possession of truth, but through its pursuit, that his powers are enlarged and it is in this alone that his ever-growing perfection lies."[6]

In a lecture in Hamburg she gave after receiving the Lessing Prize in 1959, Hannah Arendt quoted from Lessing's *Rejoinder*, citing it as an example of his concept of tolerance: "Lessing's greatness does not merely consist in a theoretical insight that there cannot be one single truth within the human world but in his gladness that it does not exist and that, therefore, the unending discourse among men will never cease so long as there are men at all." Arendt points out Lessing's conviction that "a single absolute truth . . . would have been the death of all . . . disputes,"[7] which explains why Lessing—as he maintains in his *Hamburg Dramaturgy*—only wants to sow "fermenta cognitionis," that is, according to Arendt, "to stimulate others to independent thought, and this for no other purpose than to bring about a discourse between thinkers."[8] Arendt's image of Lessing is clearly characterized by her own historical experience and hope. From this perspective the nineteenth century, with its "obsession with history and commitment to ideology"[9]—and of course also the Third Reich—obstructs the access to Lessing's heritage. In Arendt's version, philosophical postmodernism has found a trailblazer in Lessing, and so it is no surprise that a skeptic such as Richard Rorty would later write that he prefers "Lessing's choice of the infinite *striving for* truth over 'all of Truth.'"[10]

Lessing's drama of tolerance, *Nathan the Wise* (1799), is also characterized by postmodern thought *avant la lettre* when it declines to answer which is the best of all religions: The best religion is the one that makes its adherents "loved . . . in sight of God and man." The answer given here is conceived as provisional and revocable because temporal deferral can change it when, in the competition for the hearts of the majority, another religion takes the lead. Lessing's preference for the *search* for truth in *Nathan* is visible even when the judge in the Parable of the Ring indefinitely defers the decision about the true ring, or when Nathan comments on Saladin's question regarding the true religion with the words: "And now it seems that what he wants is Truth! And wants it, too, as prompt and plump as if Truth were a minted coin" (3.6). What Nathan—and Lessing—refuses is the numerical value assigned to the coin; accepting it would name a winner.

Lessing's position is interesting in our context because it highlights the shift from a process-oriented to a result-oriented approach to knowledge. While for Lessing "the honest effort he has made to get at the truth, constitutes a human being's worth," the value of the current management of knowledge lies in access to information as quickly and easily as possible. This is why texts are expected to have an abstract or a teaser, and this is why the app Summly is worth even more than what Nick D'Aloisio received for it. The desire for immediate access to condensed information is also the reason that newspaper publishers request money from Google and other news aggregators in exchange for the referrals to their contents instead of being grateful for links. A link no longer links if its text already contains everything that the reader wants to know, that is, the event as such rather than the circumstances or the possible contextual points of view.

Another well-known example of this shift from process to result is the way that Google Maps and Apple Maps encourage a user unfamiliar with an area to focus her interest only on the next street. The specification of a destination is enough to reach it; there is no need to study the map and orient oneself. This "liberation" from any information that does not serve a direct purpose is taking place on a grand scale through the use of search engines. The pointedly targeted query, bypassing threads of argumentation and associational chains (facilitated by Instant Search), reduces every book, every essay, to the index of its core statements. It passes over the process of thinking and leads directly to the supposed product of that thinking, just as Google Maps and Apple Maps lead to a destination without providing any sense of orientation. Resembling the disposition of the contemporary traveler—overly reliant on travel technology—an ignorance with respect to the "landscape" of thought seems to overcome space and time. Being on the road—the state that, for Lessing, was the meaning of a journey—has given way to arrival. There is neither space nor experience between A and B—only time reduced to (milli)seconds by the search engine that—if used for the start- and endpoint of the search—is the negation of the text as a web and of the quest for knowledge as a process. At the same time, in that it makes connections between discrete catchwords, it is the nanopublication of navigation.

Does the "the unending discourse among men" that Arendt noted as the pragmatic impetus of Lessing's skepticism with respect to truth necessarily end when we deal with knowledge in the mode of linked data? One may easily propose a contrary expectation. Knowledge, specifically in the era of the net, more easily takes on "the form of a permanent discussion" because, on the one hand, it is no longer presented as stable and, on the other, it emerges in an uncontrolled way.[11] The circumstances noted here are familiar. Nothing can be "taken home" in plain black and white. The expertocrats are drowning in the "wisdom" of the many. Weinberger's proclamation of the new process orientation of knowledge gains support with the widespread conjectures in science and technology studies and in cultural studies. And what could better exemplify these circumstances than Wikipedia, which replaces the stabilization of knowledge in the traditional encyclopedia with ceaseless volatility? But here it should be noted that the experience of contingency becomes not so much tangible as it is "lookupable." While the history of entries can be looked up, along with the discussion of any changes listed in the background, because of the monopoly that Wikipedia represents, there exists, in actuality, only *one* encyclopedia for all, with only *one* entry on a specific subject. Besides, if one reads Weinberger together with Lessing and Adorno, the conclusions are inverted since then the process is imagined not mechanically (as a new ordering of the data) but psychologically (as the ethos with respect to knowledge access). It is precisely the processes of orientation during gradual realization and becoming aware that are lost as an experience.[12]

It is possible to argue in favor of process and multiple perspectives on the Internet by making, for example, the contingency of glossaries, taxonomies, and ontologies part and parcel of the interaction with semantically annotated information. However, it is debatable to what extent this understanding of the ("raw," credible) data as (context-sensitive) statements (that can be relativized) can be implemented within the conceptual frame of the semantic web—and whether this is even desirable. Conversely, practice shows that information that has been extracted often (for example, by Wikipedia in the case of DBpedia.org) is being invisibly entered into other contexts with no effort made to make its provenance known: how this information was generated or in what context.

One should remain skeptical when Weinberger maintains that "the new medium of knowledge is less a system for the publication of articles or books; it is a networked public sphere."[13] To what extent does the opening of discourses simultaneously demand the end of the article and book as forms of discourse? How are the form of and access to publication interconnected? One possible answer lies in the link between forms of publication and their reception. Did hyperreading—as an Internet-induced model for reading after the advent of the smart phone—change our approach to knowledge to such an extent already that for *all* reading—and for the production of longer texts in particular—the necessary concentration and synthesizing power hardly exist any longer? This is precisely the accusation being made from different sources—in its most popular form by Nicholas Carr's *The Shallows: How the Internet Is Changing the Way We Think, Read, and Remember* (2010) and with radical sociopolitical critique in Bernard Stiegler's *Taking Care of Youth and the Generations* (2010). In both cases the underlying belief is that the Internet's techniques of reception favor inattentive information processing over complex thinking and thus encourage alertness to manifold stimuli without reflection. In light of its connection to hypertext, the cultural technique of surfing on the net has generated a kind of apprehension that was already recognized before Web 2.0: "Our concerns are largely limited to discrete data of information at best. Knowledge in its true sense, let alone wisdom, never really enters the equation."[14]

One can certainly agree with the findings of this undoubtedly culture-pessimistic perspective but not necessarily with its assessment. Perhaps the point of this lack of attention lies precisely in a supposed performance of Lessing's task—subverting the narcissistic truth pathos, but in a completely different way? Dissecting knowledge into its smallest units—"discrete data," in the quoted text, or "raw data" in the video cited at data.europeana.eu—also constitutes a countermovement to the constructions of grand narratives. Even if the decline in attention to the complexity and the interwoven characteristic of information posits a trust based on numbers and data quite apart from narrative interweaving, one could argue that such trust should no longer be ideologically exploited. Data love is the thirst for knowledge without the drive for narrative. It takes its truth as the face value of a coin or, more precisely, as a whole collection of loose change that hardly ever adds up to any bills with which one might engage in a significant exchange. From the perspective of memory theory, this means, simultaneously, that the situational focus of the juggler of knowledge undermines the possibility of collective memory. The collective memory that mediates the binding values and perspectives of a cultural or national group of people gives way to an "autological memory."[15] Collective memory withers away as it is overwhelmed by the individualized, situative linkage of knowledge generated by the unholy alliance of hyperlink and search machine. The result is the disappearance of retained memory in favor of functional memory that is no longer social. But from these circumstances there might emerge a "depth of superficiality" that might indeed be discussed, from a postmodern perspective, in terms of cultural optimism.[16]

PART IV

RESISTANCES

15

GOD'S EYE

SHOULD one happen to search the Internet for pictures of "computers," a series of cartoons will appear showing computers with faces and arms. Often the face is smiling while the arms wave invitingly. In one case the computer is standing at attention, holding a piece of paper and a pen, an image that at different points in time might have inspired different interpretations. Twenty, thirty years ago it might have seemed to be alluding to the possibility of a new electronic secretary or to our new paperless writing processes. In the era of Web 2.0 and big data, one might well interpret the image instead as a computer noting everything that we do, be it typed or clicked on: opening a website, viewing a video, sharing a link, dialing a number, buying a book, shortening a URL, retweeting a tweet. The "note-taking" computer has metamorphosed from an electronic secretary into a digital panopticon. Just as in Jeremy Bentham's nineteenth-century concept of the prison, in which a single guard was able to look into each cell from his tower without being seen, our activities in the net today are potentially and perpetually the object of observation. Since laptops and smart phones exist, everyone, as Zygmunt Bauman puts it, carries, just as "snails carry their homes," her own "mobile, portable single-person mini-panopticon."[1]

The metaphor of the panopticon is almost inevitable in the context of the current discourse of surveillance. However, it is only obliquely useful because the analogy of the net and the panopticon is lacking both in spatial and in temporal terms. For one thing, there is no local and hierarchical separation of the monitored inhabitants within their individual cells from the invisible guard who surveys all: on the Internet everyone can monitor everyone else without any previous sentencing or detention that would legitimize or facilitate this activity. If there is a watchman left in this constellation, a watchman who knows everything about everyone, then it is the algorithm. Second, this watchman is not required to detect any possible misconduct of those controlled in real time since whatever happens on the Internet is also stored and can be monitored after the fact. This asynchronous responsiveness is moreover an unavoidable necessity of the searching procedure: before something can be googled it has to have been stored.

For these reasons and others, surveillance research has introduced terms that modernize our conception of the panopticon with respect to digital media and their social networks. For example, "*ban*opticon" identifies unwanted groups (immigrants or unprofitable consumers, say) in order to cut off their access to certain sites, that is, to exclude them from further observation with regard to marketing. Another example is "synopticon," which indicates a reversal of the more usual act of observing: when many watch a few rather than a few watching many, that is, in the form of mass media.[2] However, the most important difference between current processes and traditional terminology lies in their function. The current panopticon does not serve to discipline; it serves to market, analyzing in order to classify.[3] It observes in the interest of customer care; it cares rather than surveils. In a way, it returns to the heart of another highly influential trope: that of the all-seeing God.

This image has its origin about four thousand years ago in the Egyptian desert into which Hagar, Abraham's slave, who was pregnant with his child, had fled to escape the fury of Abraham's wife, Sarah. In total desperation, Hagar finally experiences the appearance of an angel who commands her to return, promising many descendants. Hagar answers, "You are the God who sees me" (NIV, Genesis 16:13). The gratitude for the care that is expressed by her words lives on in Psalm 139, which invokes God as omniscient and all-caring. Later, clerical discourse will recast God's eye. It will replace the caring eye with a watchful one, the eye of the law securing the enforcement of social norms through the assertion of all-encompassing surveillance backed up by future reckoning. Bentham's panopticon and above all Foucault's discussion of it in *Discipline and Punish* secularizes this "harsh" eye of God. Google, on the other hand, as an incarnation of the all-noting computer, refers itself to the caring eye of Psalm 139: "You have searched me, LORD, and you know me."

Google's self-presentation as advisor in times of need, as an anchor point of orientation in the flood of information, operates rhetorically with a certain tendency to resacralize. It does not do so by comparing itself to God explicitly but implicitly through its unofficial company motto: "Don't be evil." This appeal excludes those business practices that, in the service of short-term gains, place the interest of customers (in the advertisement business) above that of the users (of the search engine). The biblical care presented here gains prophetic dimensions in Google's ambitions not only to answer our questions but also to tell us what we should do next.[4] Admittedly, the commitment of the search-machine giant has become a warning to all Internet users by now. It is Google's efficiency—strengthened by social and technical support in the form of tagging, login coordinates, social bookmarking, and image-recognition software—that ensures that none of our activities in the Internet remain hidden. This will be underlined all the more once Google Glass (or some similar successor technology) finally succeeds in storing and controlling our every eye movement. To the extent that Google is becoming the all-seeing eye of God, we—the Internet users, including Google's employees—have become the new chosen people of the "don't be evil" imperative. This became clearer most recently when Google's former CEO Eric Schmidt publicly declared in 2009, "If you have something that you don't want anyone to know, maybe you shouldn't be doing it in the first place," and threatened in 2010, "We know where you are. We know where you've been. We can more or less know what you're thinking about."[5]

In consumer society, care is expressed in the form of customer care, realized, for example, by way of Google's scrutiny of its users and through various forms of big-data mining. The object of data love—according to the formula quoted at the outset—is always the human being behind all the data and the enhancement of his or her economic, social, or health situation. One doesn't have to be an adherent of critical theory in order to object to the many unknowns in this formula. On which conception of the human being is this love based? Which economic improvement, and at what price? Which economic interests are involved? What constitutes social progress? What alternatives are there? Even when dealing with traffic control and healthcare the matter is not straightforward. Not everyone is ready to divulge information about their movements, even anonymously, and not everyone wants to know about their predisposition to this or that illness. But it becomes truly questionable when data analysis is performed under the banner of consumption and when data protection is compromised for this reason. A side effect of this process, which is hardly surprising, is the semiotic hostage taking of old anxiety concepts like "Big Brother," which for many today represents no more than a reality-television program.

Against this background, snooping around in social networks can only ever be seen as a trivial offense, as long as it is in the interest of enhancing customer loyalty. The surprise campaign by the Dutch airline KLM is an early example. In November 2010 it gave out little presents to its passengers before their departure: a heart-rate monitor for the lady who wanted to climb mountains, a New York City guidebook for someone who wanted to visit New York. These were personalized presents made possible by KLM checking out customers' Twitter and Facebook profiles: KLM knew the travel plans and the personal interests of the individual passengers sitting in its airplanes. It was a very successful campaign and earned KLM the epithets "cool" and "media competent." There was no mention of Big Brother.

The next step in this direction was a changing perspective with regard to Big Brother's toolset. In the 2013 Super Bowl commercial "Security Cameras," Coca-Cola flipped the negative image of surveillance cameras by turning them into witnesses of goodwill. Now they capture surprising and moving scenes: "music addicts" (the caption for a man who dances uninhibitedly in front of street musicians), "people stealing kisses" (a couple on a bench, the boy spontaneously kissing the girl), "friendly gangs" (four Arab men helping jumpstart a car), "rebels with a cause" (someone holds up a poster that reads "NO TO RACISM"), etc. With their ironic allusions to typical subjects of surveillance ("addicts," "stealing," "gangs," "rebels"), the little microcosms of these scenes achieve what the commercial as a whole aims to do: the reinterpretation of fear-laden terms and symbols as sympathetic. This reinterpretation is reinforced by Supertramp's superhit "Give a Little Bit," with a pointed readjustment of its central line: "Now's the time that we need to share / So find yourself" becomes "Now's the time that we need to share / So send a smile." In place of self-discovery we are supposed to smile for the surveillance camera. This somewhat off-beat, sugarcoated perspective on the problem of surveillance perfectly exemplifies Coca-Cola's maxim "think different" and thus assumes a mask of cool contemporaneity. However, in this context, its pseudosubversive cool plumbs the depths of cynicism.[6]

But this is exactly the rhetorical context needed by big-data business. Parallel with the defusing of fear-laden terms came the ideological exploitation of concepts with politically positive connotations like "social," "share," "transparency," "public sphere," "participation," etc. Facebook Inc.'s decision in October 2013 to allow young people between thirteen and seventeen to share their Facebook sites with all Facebook users instead of just their friends or friends of friends is an example. The purpose of doing this can hardly be mistaken. It was to open channels of communication between a potential consumer group and commercial interests while the group was still easy to influence. Outwardly, Facebook, Inc., proclaims that young people should be given more credit for self-determination and prudent behavior, and this stance is accompanied by the argument that one should offer, especially to socially active teenagers such as musicians and "humanitarian activists," the same unlimited access to the public sphere as do Twitter and Weblogs. Who would want to deny the activists among teenagers necessary access to a public sphere? This is how youth protection, educators, and child psychologists who argue with respect to the immaturity of those whom they want to protect are checkmated: by political correctness in the service of the market economy.

16

DATA HACKS

T HE question still remains: What can be done about the situation of data analysis and dwindling data protection? The most urgent and simple answer is to educate people concerning the technical aspects and social effects of data mining. The former develops media literacy, with the primary goal being to become better informed about what data is collected, when and how, and also how this might be prevented or at least controlled. Media literacy here includes encryption methods as well as familiarity with alternative software, the ability to change the basic settings of an application, and the competence to analyze data on one's own. This pragmatic part of media literacy concerns the "I" in media. The question of the "us" in media is addressed by the political and cultural contextualization of technological development. It aims at a broad social discussion of the secret decisions and hidden struggles taking place before the new social models and cultural practices are fully established. This kind of media literacy fosters competence in reflection, and, as we have seen, it may take its point of departure from older texts—be it Bacon's *Nova Atlantis*, Bentham's *Panopticon*, Lessing's *Rejoinder*, Chamisso's *Schlemihl*, Dürrenmatt's *Physicians*, or the story of Hagar in the Old Testament.[1]

The matter becomes so complex and hopeless because data mining is not only about a battle between citizens and the intelligence agencies or actual governmental authorities but also about the relationship between citizens and businesses. One can say very little against the transparent man if he is produced in the interests of customer service. But then it must be shown to be the case that this customer service is indeed in the customer's interest. Whether it is or not is brought into question under the rubric of "filter bubble" with regard to Facebook's algorithms of personalization, and the question arises again when we consider customized books and films as future products of perception mining.

The proposal that rather than buying what they want (or should want) customers get what a business wants to sell them is the basic idea in Hans Weingartner's film *Free Rainer—Dein Fernseher lügt* (Free Rainer—your TV is lying, 2007). A successful, cynical TV producer has a revelation: "No viewer is as stupid as the shows we produce." Since his boss considers the audience an "opportunistic horde" and has the viewer ratings on his side, Rainer's rebellion begins with data analysis: the rating box "that decides on everything in this country." Faking the ratings—raising them for channels such as PBS, lowering them for those like Fox—makes the TV stations (and this was the plan) produce more sophisticated programs. The big surprise—and idealistic confirmation of the earlier defense of the viewers—lies in the fact that the ratings for quality programs rise even after the police have discovered and stopped the manipulation. A headline in the film announces triumphantly, "The Rating Revolution Continues." Encouraged by this success, Rainer's support group moves on to Hasloh, a village with a representative population sample where retail businesses are testing consumer behavior. The end of the film shows the data forgers at the cash register of a supermarket, where—during the reading of customers' cards—they delete all the goods from the list that are, among groceries, what trash is in the TV world: potato chips, Coke Light, diet pills.

This is an example of how, in the context of data mining, criticism of the culture industry presents as pop culture: liberation of customers through data fraud. True to the characteristic style of critical theory, Weingartner's heroes own up to their self-image as smart-aleck social engineers. They want to free the masses from all forms of fast food, even against their will if necessary, since—and this is an axiom of the culture-industry thesis—their will has already been manipulated by powerful corporations. The resistance is more democratic when the distortion of data is carried out by the data's actual sources, as for example when several people use the very same discount card and thus harvest price deductions without delivering reliable data. Another option, that of obfuscating data, one also demanding less logistical effort, is Steve Klise's I Like What I See, an app for Google's browser, Chrome, which automatically clicks all "like" buttons on each page visited, or the similar browser extension AdNauseam, by Helen Nissenbaum, Daniel Howe, and Mushon Zer-Aviv.[2]

More drastic than the model of sabotage is that of boycott. It is more drastic because it abstains from media in a society that is media saturated. In a more moderate form, this boycott takes place through the use of alternative means of communication—using, for example, the e-mail of an independent server instead of Facebook's messenger—and thus evading big-data mining.[3] The most commonly discussed form of data evasion is encryption, on which Julian Assange and his coauthors rely as the ultimate form of nonviolent resistance in their book *Cypherpunks: Freedom and the Future of the Internet* (2012). Of course, encryption is useless if Trojan viral programs have obtained access before sending (encoding) or after receiving (decoding). However, setting aside any weaknesses of this procedure, it suffers—similarly to other forms of boycott and sabotage—from an internal contradiction: the fight for the right to cryptography will only reach as far as the disinterest of the individuals with regard to all the advantages that Web 2.0 transparency has to offer. Those who want to use Facebook's and Google's services without restrictions will have to give these services all the necessary data—and will do so without much reluctance.

Boycott becomes more radical when people self-experiment with media abstinence under a slogan like "My six months offline." For some time such titles on reports and books have been selling as well as the reports on "the Internet and me" did twenty years ago. Life without the Internet and mobile phone is reminiscent of the officially restricted zones that Werner Sombart advocated in his 1935

essay "Die Zähmung der Technik" (The taming of technology)—
both natural and cultural reservations without cars and factories:
spaces that preserve a bygone era. Current variations of technology-
denial conceive of such reserved regions merely in terms of distinct
time slots during which electronic devices remain turned off. On
the whole, the results of this self-experimentation show that there is
as little interest in living permanently "off the grid" as there was for
dwelling in Sombart's artificial natural spaces.

Another approach to dealing with the unwanted consequences
of measurement simply advocates more advanced methods of measuring. Jennifer Golbeck, director of the Human-Computer Interaction Lab at the University of Maryland, suggested this in a TED
talk in 2013. Since one can hardly expect effective action for data
protection from politics, science is supposed to provide more of that
action by pointing out the consequences of its activities to users:
"By liking this Facebook page or by sharing this piece of personal
information you've now improved my ability to predict whether or
not you are using drugs or whether or not you get along well in the
work place."[4] By suggesting this, the data scientists—whose mechanisms of analysis are creating the privacy problem in the first place,
a fact that Golbeck is in no way concealing—are more or less rec-
ommending themselves as the best solution to the problem, opting
for an increase in the dose of data-analysis therapy, so to speak. This
procedure will reassure only those who believe in the independence
of science from economics and who consider the information on
their original "like" and "share" impulses safe with the scientists.

Conceptually, Golbeck's suggestion may be compared with
attempting to cure the unwanted effects of a technology by introducing an alternative technology. The photo-sharing app Snapchat
seems to be a hopeful example of this symptomatic condition since
it deletes the photos it sends a few seconds after they have been
opened. The former Stanford students Bobby Murphy and Evan
Spiegel had this idea in 2011, the year in which Viktor Mayer-
Schönberger's book *Delete: The Virtue of Forgetting in the Digital Age*
was published. That something had to be done against the unrelent-
ing memory of the Internet had long been perfectly clear to many.

The trinity of smart phone, Internet, and search engine relies on the ability to store, and the value of everything that is stored hinges on the ability to find it. Some people—one has learned over time—have even lost their jobs or failed to get one because disreputable photos and texts by or about them appeared on the wrong monitors. Because of this, the CEO of Google, Eric Schmidt, suggested that one should be allowed to change one's name after reaching the legal age of maturity. This was meant seriously, if not entirely sincerely, since Google could easily create a connection between the old and the new identity. It seemed more reasonable to supply one's photos and texts with an expiration date, although how to do this practically remained unclear. However, it was only a matter of time before someone developed an application like Snapchat that now applies the impermanence with which photos are made and shared to the processes of reception.

It was only a question of time before Facebook and Google wanted to own Snapchat—offering three and four billion dollars respectively. They did not succeed in their ambition. It seems that Murphy and Spiegel also know—as did, at the time, Mark Zuckerberg, who in 2006 spurned Yahoo's offer to sell Facebook for a billion dollars—that their app is worth more. What would the two Internet giants have done with the Snapchat app, an app that subverts both Facebook's concept of archiving and Google's search engine? Would they have locked it in a safe? Basically, Snapchat is stabbing Google in its back. Around the time when Google's Glass project promised to digitize every glance in the analogue world, Snapchat, by contrast, subordinated the digital photo to the rules of an analogue world. Memory is stored only in the human mind, far from any possibilities of accumulation and analysis. This means that the adages of earlier media are once again in play: "Tell me what you *remember*, and I will tell you who you are," and media theory is enriched by one more paradox: "Oralize" the image, and it will fade away as fast as the spoken word.

However, addressing the question of why Murphy and Spiegel did not sell is of even more importance. Is it idealism that makes them turn down Facebook and Google? Do they foresee a business whose value greatly surpasses the billions offered? The fact that Snapchat is preferred for "sexting"—the sending of sexual self-ies—points to one of the most profitable markets in the world. The ephemerality of sexual activity and communication has an appeal beyond the bounds of licentious youth culture—and precisely when that which has vanished or been withdrawn can no longer be forgotten, the name of the app (a pun on the word snapshot) develops its dialectic potential as a persistent reference to evacuated moments. An alternative business model—which is shady only in an ideological sense—might be to transform every Snapchat photo into a promotional image offering a special thrill: the content would be tailor made for its recipient, sender, or portrait subject. A more honorable model would be produced by the development of a market in the protection of data, something for which a great future has been predicted. In the visual realm, Snapchat promises to make the digital more ephemeral, and this seems to be the best remedy against the data measurement of the private realm. The fact that this move begins with the visual shows to what extent Snapchat is up to date. It is in the realm of visuality that big-data mining's future areas of prospecting lie. The question is whether Snapchat will also serve as a model for complementary protocols guiding the destruction of data in the realm of textual communication. The four billion dollars recently refused would surely be recouped as soon as Snapchat, as a "merriamwebsterable" key technology, was able to guarantee a worldwide "right to forget."

But all these variations are put forward with far too much naivety once we consider what Snapchat really stands for. One has to take the name seriously in order to understand how this medium alters the human situation. Snapchat is, in truth, a new form of *chat*ting, but no longer in the terms of SMS, WhatsApp, or other text messengers; it functions via photo dialogue. One does not text that one is going to the movies—instead one sends a Snapchat of the entrance to the theater. One does not write about how one is doing—instead one sends a selfie in front of the TV with a drink, feet up, on the coffee table. Snapchat not only changes the way in which photos are made and shared; it also invites you to replace verbal communication with photographs, and it then goes further: the deletion of the photos gives us back the ephemerality of oral communication. Snapchat thus promotes the transition—and in terms of media history a return—from the symbolic practices of language to a "language" of visuality that the media philosopher Vilém Flusser predicted as part of the development of digital media in the 1980s.[5]

With regard to cognitive theory, this transition can be seen as problematic since it replaces a reflexive communication model of language with an associative model applied to images. The sender's sovereignty over information is reduced from choosing the words that describe a situation simply to choosing the situation that is proposed for description. In other words, one only has to decide whether a certain moment should be transmitted in a Snapchat or not. In line with the "like" or the "share" without commentary, this is another example of how digital media's binary model of operation is established on our side of the interface as a cultural formation. From a less critical perspective, this mode of communication might be considered to be more intimate. Since an image is worth a thousand words, the Snapchat image allows the receiver to decode the message by focusing on a certain detail, which in its turn will serve as the content of the reply. Thus, on the basis of mutually shared knowledge, the images can operate as the syntactic elements of a nonverbal but linear conversation. This allows us to view Snapchat as, at least potentially, an inspiring form of communication with ample room for wit and subtle references.

However, the transition from linguistic to visual communication is problematic in the context of data mining not only because ephemerality is illusory given the existence of apps and tricks to capture Snapchat images but also because this change of communicative media entails the acquisition of additional levels and quantities of information. The Snapchat photo embeds all the usual metadata: for example, precise information on place and time of its origin. Consequently, the Snapchat provider accumulates an enormous trove of knowledge if it retains the metadata, including the photographs themselves, even after their removal from the screens and devices of the recipient. This is all the more a treasure trove because it is much more reliable as compared to, at least, the body of communication by text. The text message—"just saw a really cool Armani dress"—is not as data rich even if it contains the location and date of its sending because it is not necessarily tied to the place and the moment of its production. It could also have been written later in the subway. A photo, on the other hand, is tied to the scene of the event and reveals exactly when and in which branch of a store a particular dress attracted attention—and even the photograph's focus on certain details could be of interest. The "optical unconscious" a photograph reveals provides more information than the photographer intended to share.[6] Viewed in this manner, Snapchat promises, superficially, to make information more ephemeral while effectively feeding additional information to big-data mining. It is precisely here that its relevance for the future lies: It casts out the devil with Beelzebub while rendering itself the most effective Trojan horse for the data miners—this is easily worth a great deal more than four billion dollars.

What can we hope for, if boycott is not an alternative and neither are the so-called alternative technologies themselves? Do we have to accept the inevitable and start thinking about making appropriate adjustments? Sometimes old rights and expectations simply can't be enforced against new media. A famous example is that of the Catholic Church losing its hermeneutic monopoly after Gutenberg invented the printing press with movable type, which soon, especially after Luther's translation into vernacular, made the Bible accessible for many believers. Today we experience a similar situation. Privacy as we once knew it cannot be preserved in the context of new technologies and the new cultural habits they bring with them.

If forgetting can no longer be secured on the Internet, we need a new culture of forgiving. This is one of the proposals to be found in the public debate. If anybody can know everything about anybody else, then we have to approach the skeletons in our closet differently. This formula seems plausible. After all, how could anyone campaign with moral conviction against adultery or homosexuality if data reveal them to be ubiquitous phenomena? This is the good side of statistics. They unmask and normalize so-called misdoings as run-of-the-mill social practices. However, a different approach requires public debate tackling all these "misdoings" and "skeletons" head on. A good place to start would be ensuring that foolish displays on social networks of such things as excessive adolescent drinking or cannabis consumption should not affect job interviews or that the love affairs of politicians need not be taken as a damning commentary on professional competence. To be sure, there will be counter-arguments put forward by those whose skeletons are less terrifying or simply different and by those who, with the exact same skeletons in their cupboard, manage to fly under the radar. The response to big data and data love has to begin not only with legal reform but also and first of all with an updating of social norms. The self-directed reassurance "he who has nothing to hide has nothing to fear" must be strengthened and humanized: "Because I can't hide anything anymore, I don't want to fear what is human." The discussion on big data demands a discussion of the human condition.

At the end of their report about the opportunities and challenges of big-data mining, Mayer-Schönberger and Cukier propose the generation of the "algorithmists": "experts in the areas of computer science, mathematics, and statistics" who would act as "reviewers of big-data analyses and predictions."[7] As a blend of management consultancy and consumer-protection agency, algorithmists would "vet big-data analysis for integrity and accuracy before letting them go live" and serve as contacts for anybody "who feels harmed by organizations' big-data predictions."[8] This proposal is in line with considerations about "Corporate Technical Responsibility": the voluntary commitment of IT corporations to take responsibility for the social, economic, and political implications of their technical innovations.[9] It remains to be seen how pragmatic such self-regulation would be and how competent the algorithmists would prove themselves to be in engaging not only with the legal but also with the moral discussion of the relevant issues. While the outcome would certainly be affected by their training, it is doubtful that moral issues can be delegated to a new class of experts. Statistics, which will be a central focus of the algorithmists' work, can provide progressive arguments in favor of behavior and conduct that is currently socially unacceptable, but they can do so only within the paradigm of quantification. The question becomes how society will treat "misdoings" that have, as yet, no majority behind them, as was the situation for homosexuality a hundred years ago and for autopsies in the Middle Ages. In the age of an inevitable transparency, should individual conduct be morally evaluated on the basis of numbers? Should Rousseau's numerical-mathematic rationality prevail over Condorcet's communicative-discursive rationality? The way the question is framed reveals that the moral issues underlying the practices of big data are also political issues.

The political dimension comes into focus when transparency is conceptualized as political enlightenment. The classical example in the realm of the Internet is WikiLeaks; another is LobbyPlag.eu, which tracks interventions by lobbyists (originally those advocating for weak privacy laws) in amendments by members of the European Parliament. In a similar vein, theyrule.net by Josh On visualizes—with names and biographical details available online—the interrelations via individuals among the boards of powerful U.S. companies and institutions. If one adapts this procedure to the era of big data, with the enhancements of face-recognition software and augmented reality, then it is not unlikely that soon everybody will be transparent to everyone else in every respect. Maybe there will be filters allowing us to focus on profession, wealth, family situation, love affairs, and so on. The filter of theyrule.net 2.0 would probably target the political implications. How did the person in front of you make his or her money? How much did he or she pay for their sneakers or their jewelry? How many children have spent how many hours in sweatshops and gold mines to produce these goods? Which party does this person vote for, and who works with his or her money?

Would this kind of transparency be the payoff for offering up one's own individual transparency? Would this amount to the ennoblement of an evil technology? When the rich and powerful can no longer hide, the feeling of satisfaction at their getting their just deserts is undeniable. But the nightmare of the transparent subject exists above party lines or not at all. In any case it is clear that big data is not a problem for software engineers, lawmakers, or algorithmists. It requires a political and moral debate. Starting this debate is in the interest of all those who regard current technological development with deep discontent yet are too intelligent or sensitive to believe that whatever threat there is can be overcome by sabotage, boycott, or better technology.

17

ON THE RIGHT LIFE
IN THE WRONG ONE

"There Is No Analogue Life in the Digital One" was to be the title of one chapter in Michael Seemann's publication project *Das neue Spiel—Strategien für die Welt nach dem digitalen Kontrollverlust* (The new game—Strategies for the world after the digital loss of control), when it was announced before its release in the fall of 2014. It was safe to assume that this chapter would have established that one can no longer withdraw into analogue culture in the era of digital technologies—on the one hand, because one would then be deprived of many possibilities for communication while, on the other, because such a "safe haven" no longer even exists. The digital realm is everywhere—only hermits deny this, and then only until they meet someone with a smart phone in the forest.

Of course, the chapter title remains interesting despite these banal insights because of its allusion to Adorno's infamous saying: "There is no right life in the wrong one." The saying is notorious because it insinuates that we live in a time that has not yet accomplished human emancipation but is still completely subservient to unscrupulous production and consumption. According to Adorno, history to date has gone wrong and, in fact, has not even begun yet. To live in the wrong life means to live in the wrong social system, in the "prehistory" of human destiny. Adorno's conception of history has been characterized as out of touch with reality and complacently pessimistic, a "beautiful dream of a bad world,"[1] which would prompt intellectuals like him to call for the "emergence from man's self-incurred immaturity" in a condescending manner. But unlike Kant, who had answered the question "What is Enlightenment?" with that phrase in 1784, Adorno regards immaturity—which, according to Kant, is the "inability to use one's own understanding without the guidance of another," and today this "another" is also the algorithm—not as self-inflicted but as the consequence of social existence: lack of educational opportunity; monotonous, vapid work; and—Adorno's preferred enemy—the culture industry's strategies of distraction.

Forty-five years after Adorno's death one rarely encounters this point of view. How can one cling to Adorno's historico-philosophical conclusion in light of Francis Fukuyama's statement about the *end* of history? If there is no alternative social model to the liberal free-market economy, then an opinion concerning the wrong life is less and less convincing—or it remains valid only in the way that Winston Churchill referred to democracy as the worst form of government "except for all those other forms that have been tried from time to time." In this "wrong" life there must be the right one or, in any case, one that is "more right." This is already hinted at in Jacques Rancière's statement of the "disaster of the emancipation-promise" that is "waking us from a sleep-filled life of consumption, only to throw us headlong into the fatal utopias of totalitarianism."[2] The cynical apotheosis of inevitable disillusion can be found in the rewriting of the *Communist Manifesto* into the *consumist* one—an in no way far-fetched praise of consumerism as "pragmatic cosmopolitanism," as "global society's immune system against the virus of fanatic religions."[3] "Consumers of the world, unite!" is the battle cry upon which the owners of smart phones in both the East and West can agree. The "right life in the wrong one" can be found wherever citizens take a stand for freedom, equality, and ecology while at the same time remain convinced they live in the right social system precisely because it enables a battle for its own improvement rather than suppressing any environmental and civil-rights movement. Addressing pollution and supporting areas with reduced traffic is a part of this fight just as much as supporting immigrants and "saving" the Internet.

The purpose of this digression on Adorno is not aimed at asking whether, accepting the transmogrification of his statement, there could be an analogue life in the digital one after all. The intent is rather to reiterate the connection between technology and society: the mirroring of social conditions (consumerism) in technological structures complements the redefinition of society within the parameters of technology (computation, datafication). With this in mind, the question appears with new agencies: Is there a right technology in a wrong society? Consumerism and surveillance predominate on the Internet—this was Evgeny Morozov's answer to the survey carried out by *Die Zeit* on whether the Internet could be saved—because they predominate in modernity. Can the Internet be saved without saving society (in Adorno's sense)? Asked in this way, discussion on data protection and data love goes far beyond anything surrounding Snowden's leaks and their violation of data protection. As the end of this book circles us back to its beginning, this also means a return to critical theory.

On March 10, 2014, in a video message broadcast at the South by Southwest Festival, the thirty-year-old Edward Snowden urged programmers and software engineers to develop better means for the protection of privacy. "The NSA Set Fire to the Web, Silicon Valley Needs to Put It Out," as the *Guardian's* headline put it the following day.[4] At the same festival, one of the most well-known representatives of Silicon Valley, Google's former CEO and current CEC Eric Schmidt, spoke about the future of privacy. When he pointed out that information can no longer be kept concealed from or within Google, this was free of any signs of remorse. The incidental drawbacks could not be denied—nor were they, although he regretted the negative effects of embarrassing YouTube videos for the professional careers of teenagers. One should be armed against misuse and abuse, and therefore, Schmidt announced, Google had made its servers more secure after they were hacked by the Chinese and by the NSA. But none of this undermined his conviction that technological developments were positive in principle—last but not least because

Google embodies the advantages that a resolute and effective accumulation and analysis of data promises for its customers. Google's CEO Larry Page also underlined the advantages of big-data mining for medicine, warning against throwing the baby out with the bathwater with respect to the privacy problem. The "bathwater" in this case is the NSA and other privacy offenders; the "baby" includes corporations like Google that only want to know as much as possible about their users in order to serve their interests.[5] This perspective supports a basis of business in Silicon Valley and more particularly that associated with big data: the conviction that one is acting in the interest of the individual and of society—along with a tacit agreement not to question this conviction. One might respond to Page with another saying: In matters of privacy, you can't put the fox in charge of the henhouse. But then who do you put in charge?

At the same time that Snowden and Schmidt made their appearances, Tim Berners-Lee, inventor of the World Wide Web, suggested a Magna Carta for the Internet that would anchor its structures and procedures constitutionally, thereby establishing an all-but-sovereign significance of the Internet for society. This appeal is part of the campaign "The Web We Want" that Berners-Lee and the World Wide Web Consortium he founded launched during the web's twenty-fifth anniversary. It is an appeal not only aimed at software engineers but also at political organizations, net activists, and all those for whom a "free, open, and truly global Internet" is close to their hearts. Such an approach promises more than an appeal to Silicon Valley. However, it also *overlooks* the concurrence of a majority of the population with the underlying intentions of Silicon Valley. For a great number of people, the "open and trusted" Internet promoted by "The Web We Want" means, primarily, an Internet that is accessible and reliable at all times. In other words, the same thing Google and Facebook and Amazon and many other big-data miners also need and desire.

And so, the vast majority of people will continue administering their e-mails via Gmail, hoping that Google continues reading them avidly in order to keep its promise to tell this majority of users what they should do next. They will continue not to be dissuaded from the installation of an app if it demands access to data having nothing to do with the actual function of this app. They will continue to make their GPS data public in order to receive personal messages concerning speed cameras. They will not refrain from storing personal data in the cloud in order to have unfettered access to that data everywhere at all times—because anything else would be much too complicated. If apps measure temperature, blood pressure, heart rate, and stress level, they won't be petty and ask why the data have to be sent to the cloud first, nor will they oppose sharing this data with others. If the future offers us ingestible chips to gather health data from the inside of our bodies, the majority will swallow the chips. Even after having absorbed all the warnings regarding the loss of privacy, they will not be able to resist getting excited when developers talk about refrigerators that tweet or about "open interfaces."[6]

Berners-Lee and Snowden—like many of the activists in the United States, Europe, and Germany who are appealing to us to save the Internet—are certainly not against sharing medical data nor against Google's idea of customer service. They are convinced that everyone wants the Internet for the same reasons and as much as they do, that is, not as a place of commerce and surveillance but as an interactive medium for communication to promote democracy, just as Adorno had implied that people want more than what is given to them by those in power, the culture industry, and the social status quo. The reaction to Adorno was not limited to the defiant embrace of the culture industry. He was also—justifiably—denied the right to judge individual values, from jazz to TV series. And all those who are not passionate about the Internet that is envisioned by Snowden, Berners-Lee, and other activists are equally unlikely to admit to any dishonest motives—be it stinginess and idle comfort or exhibitionism and narcissism. They will argue that the seeming disenfranchisement is in reality an emancipation; that big-data mining can solve economic, medical, and administrative problems; that the measurement of the social realm is a promising enterprise for a future that can no longer be comprehended by the old terminology of "surveillance," "control," "privacy," etc. They will silence those who conceal themselves, those who hide their data, while sounding the war cry of the Internet pioneers: "Information wants to be free!" And they won't call it the right life in the wrong one; they will call it the good life, the best of all possible lives. It is thus possible that a report from the distant future will label the Snowdens and the Berners-Lees as the Adornos of the early twenty-first century, their visions of a better, freer Internet derided or already forgotten as entirely as today we forget Adorno's dream of an emancipated society in which alienation and consumer culture are banished.

It would be a depressing conclusion if this prognosis proved to be an accurate report from the future. As a dystopian vision, however, it is an appeal to the present conscience, urging us to bring the current evolution of events to a halt. "The prophecy of a coming disaster is done in order to prevent its arrival" is how Hans Jonas once justified the assumption of the worst-case scenario.[7] Already the shift in the focus of the current debate is disappointing: from the Internet as utopia—promising a better world—to the Internet as dystopia—warning against a world that is worse. Perhaps it is necessary to have such low expectations in order to achieve anything. Disillusion is a better starting point than any wishful thinking, to which even critical considerations of the utopian potential of the new media quite often finally resort. Even conspiracy theory, à la Julian Assange, may be more productive than a sheer unshakeable belief in the goodness of humanity. If the charges are not convincing, nonetheless, by continually reminding oneself *"that* is not the way it is," the *that* is kept mindfully present, enough that it can be recognized once the state of affairs slowly begins to feel just like *that*.

EPILOGUE

SHORTLY before the release of the German edition of *Data Love*, the discussion on big data within the German media seemed to allow for a more optimistic conclusion to the book. A number of newspaper articles gave the impression that there was an increasing sensitivity to the social implications of digital technology among politicians. However, hope was not engendered by the appointed Internet commissioner, Gesche Joost, who, after one hundred days in office, displayed little enthusiasm considering the panic and the deep concern caused by Snowden's revelations. It was other politicians who called for a thorough discussion of urgent issues in the spring of 2014. Here is a brief summary of articles from the *Frankfurter Allgemeine Zeitung*, whose publisher, Frank Schirrmacher, and columnists Evgeny Morozov and Constanze Kurz had been commenting critically on digital media for some time:

On February 6, social democrat Martin Schulz, SPD politician and president of the European Parliament, warns that Internet companies and intelligence services could bring about technological totalitarianism and advocates, as a response, the determination of individual rights and a explicit policy for the Internet, with a structure similar to that for social legislation and environmental policy. On February 20, the former minister of interior, Gerhart Baum of the liberal FDP, declares the digitization of society as the one central, unavoidable item on the twenty-first-century political agenda. On March 6, the FDP chairman Christian Lindner stresses that progress must not come at the cost of irreversible restrictions to personal freedoms, demanding, with respect to the data market, "a balance of power" between users and providers. Representing the liberal party, Lindner does not forget to stress that the Internet should operate according to market-based laws.

A different and more radical tone is set by the SPD chairman and secretary of commerce Gabriel when, on May 16, he appeals for the taming of "data capitalism." At stake, he says, is nothing less than the future of democracy in the age of digitization and hence the prospects for the freedom, emancipation, participation, and self-determination of five hundred million people in Europe. These were big words calculated to appeal for consensus: Who would argue against legislation that would insure people's control over their own data? The cross-party consensus seems to end, however, when Gabriel goes on to write about the crowdsourcer and clickworker as the disenfranchised day laborer of digital modernity.[1]

Such articles promise a new sensibility among politicians, a responsiveness that is certainly thanks to Snowden's revelations but also to the complaints by German top managers about Google's misuse of its power, as well as to the criticism and claims from Internet activists and media theorists. It is possible that these warnings may have the same kind of effect as those of Adorno still sometimes evoke for those, at least, who do not see history as God given but instead as human engineered. One can only hope that the politicians' statements represent real concern and interest rather than merely an attempt to boost their profiles. One also hopes that the concerns go beyond lobbyism on behalf of German and European (Internet) companies and aim, instead, at generating widespread discussion of the cultural and social implications of technological progress. If the debate only shifts the criticism from NSA snooping to Google's monopoly, or if it is intended, as some suspect, to distract from the issue of the intelligence agencies, the chance to tackle deeper consequences of the digital revolution would be lost once more.

A significant step beyond the usual debate on privacy and fair competition is Gabriel's critical approach to crowdsourcing. This is a long-overdue response to the sunny rhetoric coming from Silicon Valley—which, incidentally, also emanates from German companies. But Gabriel's question "Who decides according to which rules we live?" should not only be understood in economic and legislative terms. Nor should one look for an answer to this question within the framework of an old model of power according to which individuals determine the rules. The discussion of such a conventional framework may be necessary, but it is also necessary to discuss the rules—or the dispositifs—that digital media establish for culture and society in the twenty-first century. To mention only three of the crucial questions that Gabriel's query triggers: How do the culture of transparency in social networks and the increasing efficiency of search engines alter our attitude toward privacy, forgetting, and forgiving? How do Google, Wikipedia, and the semantic web change our relationship to knowledge? How do hyperattention and "power browsing" modify the way we think?

All in all, the question we need to ask is one that addresses the message of the medium. What is the inner logic of digital media, and how do these media enforce this logic in the social constellation? Such a question exceeds the responsibility and competency of any ministries of economics or the interior. The hope is that all ministries participate in the discussion, perhaps even under the auspices of a new "ministry of the Internet" that had been proposed in Germany during the 2013 elections. Ideally such a new government department—in close cooperation with consultants representing both the pragmatic and the theoretical side of media literacy—would assist the Department of Education in extending the discussion to schools and universities. In these institutions, through education—and perhaps there first of all—data love must be discussed as something that is more than just fuel for the economy of the information age. It is a complex subject with far-reaching moral, political, and philosophical consequences—without doubt the most delicate and troubling love story of the twenty-first century.

POSTFACE

SINCE the German release of *Data Love* in the summer of 2014 we have experienced the further growth of this delicate and troubling love. Business models such as Airbnb and Uber expose people's travel behavior—in the city and beyond it, and not only within the United States—to the clouds of big data. The new businesses encourage us to *desire* to be good customers, for now customers themselves are rated, not just the services or goods. You are what you have been—what was long true for your credit history now applies to other fields of life as well. Thus we no longer burp in a cab and make sure to flush the toilet before we leave, afraid to be rejected the next time we need a ride or a place to stay.

Of course, we understand that we can't have Uber without a rating system. Rating is an aspect of the business model according to which Uber signals that it is not a taxi company but a communication platform facilitating the organization of people who are willing to offer other people a lift in exchange for financial compensation. Hence, it is only logical that the drivers be reviewed by their customers and—to make it more Web 2.0–like—that, in return, drivers be given the right to review their customers also. The more implicit demand that we disclose more data about our private lives comes, again, as a function of services that we can't resist. Particularly in Hong Kong, from where the author writes, one appreciates a car that isn't rundown, dirty, and way too cold. But the appeal goes deeper and applies everywhere. We enjoy knowing beforehand, we don't want to play it by ear, we don't like surprises. With Uber we know the driver's name before she or he arrives, and with the new integrated Spotify app we can even determine the music that will be playing before we get into the car. In return we pay with data: when, from where, to where, how often—and our taste in music. We don't mind this, as long as it buys us more convenience, and we hope—as usual—that nobody will reveal or misuse our data. This is a hope that has lost some ground recently when AshleyMadison was hacked in the summer of 2015 and much sensitive data concerning "love" was made public.

Since the release of *Data Love* in Europe, the passage of time has shown that its optimistic ending was premature. A wide-ranging discussion on the cultural implications of digital technology did not occur in Germany. Neither did it occur in the other European countries, nor in the United States. The appointment of a German ambassador for the Internet didn't help in this regard, which is not surprising given the description of the corresponding European-level organization, a board of "Digital Champions" created by the European Union in 2012. Their main program—as "ambassadors for the Digital Agenda, appointed by their Member States to help every European become digital"—is to "actively promote the development of digital skills and entrepreneurship by young people, helping tackle youth unemployment by sharing innovative ideas which have worked in their own country."[1] Regrettably, the issues taken up are not the increasing transparency and quantification of human behavior, the growing commercialization and algorithmic regulation of the Internet, or the loss of deep attention. Rather the issues are network development, network neutrality, data protection, and copyright. Thus, these ambassadors campaign for free access to the Internet without dead spots and exclusion (for example, on behalf of people with dementia, stroke patients, or the hearing or visually impaired), for the protection of intellectual property, for e-learning and employability. In line with this framework the German ambassador does not plan to question "becoming digital" but simply calls for more programming classes in primary schools.

It is not that there is anything to be said against the development of practical skills—as long as the efficient use of digital media does not position itself against a vital critical reflection concerning their social implications.

To be fair, the German government is quite aware of the risks posed by the digital revolution. As was to be expected, the government's 2014 *Digital Agenda*—meant to "seize the opportunities that digitization presents to strengthen Germany's role as an innovative and highly productive economy within the European Union and across the globe"—embraces all the innovations and new business made possible by digital technologies and repeatedly drops the names of all the trending buzzwords: "Industry 4.0, 3D, smart services, big data and cloud computing."[2] Crowdsourcing—which Gabriel calls in his newspaper article "the day labor of digital modernity"—is now addressed as one of the "new working arrangements" that should not be allowed to undermine, as a veiled warning tells us, a "high level of occupational health and safety for employees."

Nonetheless, the document also speaks of risks and threats associated with the positive effects of digitization: "the ever increasing volume of digital information . . . can be used by organizations to make predictions about people's everyday habits and behaviors in a way that was never before possible. This use of data is based on the storage and analysis of huge volumes of data and may have serious implications for freedom of action and the protection of privacy." Hence, the German government also promotes "the social and political debate surrounding the relationship between freedom and security and the private and the public sphere" and is "committed to a high level of data protection that continues to guarantee the freedom and right to privacy of citizens."[3] Aspects of this commitment include support for the establishment of an "Internet arbitration board" and a "watchdog to monitor the digital world," the introduction of the "right of associations to take legal action to improve data protection," as well as the demand for "technology-based data protection (privacy by design) and privacy-friendly default settings (privacy by default)."

This may look like a great deal of consumer protection compared to that in the United States and other countries. It remains to be seen how successful the German government will be in its aspirations "to be in the vanguard of the development of international data protection principles."[4] Shall we hope to see that Germany's comparatively radical advocacy of privacy prevails? Will it harm Germany's economy, as the chairman of the German Bitkom (Federal Association for Information Technology, Telecommunications, and New Media) Thorsten Dirks—who is also the CEO of Telefónica Germany—predicted in July 2015? In his comment on the first anniversary of *Digital Agenda*, Dirks considers the high data-protection regulations in Germany a hindrance for innovative business models and warns that only generous access to user data will guarantee Germany's success in the digital revolution. We must not apply the rules of the analog world to one in the digital economy, he tells us: we must review the concept of data thriftiness; we must become more daring. It is not surprising that politicians, including the German chancellor, are repeating this kind of warning, pointing out that data are the resources of the future and that they need to be retrieved if Germany does not want to degenerate into merely the workbench for other countries' economies.[5]

The conflict is one between economy and opportunity, on the one hand, and social values, on the other hand. This is a conflict that resides, implicitly, in the heart of *Digital Agenda*, as becomes clear if certain passages are brought together. There is the intention to become a frontrunner in the new field—"We want Germany to become Europe's number-one country for digital growth"—but also to hold on to old values—"we must continue to ensure that our existing value systems are not lost in the digital world, and that they continue to provide a framework for our future coexistence."[6] The government is aware of the conflict and tries to resolve the differences: "The technology-neutral nature of our existing system of values allows sufficient flexibility for new technological developments. Amendments are only required where existing law fails to cover new developments or where a lack of enforcement arises." The delusion—or denial—is belied by the word "only" when we consider how many traditional customs and laws have given way to the realities of digital culture: from copyright and cybercrime to youth protection and antitrust law. In practice, almost everything needs to be adjusted if everything is digitized.

The business world already knows this and acts accordingly. Politicians will soon learn their lessons and give in. Some of them, no doubt, are already in the know. If, for example, the government—under the rationale of "environmental awareness in the use of IT" (in the German version: "Green durch [through- R.S.] IT")—aims at the "implementation of smart metering systems for consumers, producers, and water heaters" and at the expanding of the "eHealth initiative, enhancing links with the innovations delivered by health-care businesses"—what is it talking about if not the data-mined citizen, the transparent citizen?[7] Will people be able to reject metering systems that know exactly when and how many of them are at home if the protection of the environment is taken to be a bigger cause than the protection of privacy? Will they be *allowed* to opt out once the authorities are convinced that data collection benefits both the individual and the national body by improving health and rendering financial support more efficient?

It is the government itself that will undermine the cultural norms it purports to protect by making accommodations with digital "realities" and opportunities. It will, as it states, "promote business models that use anonymisation and pseudonymization measures" and "help companies improve their IT security."[8] But how secure are anonymizations? These days we know that reidentification is easy! And how reassuring is a promise "to ensure that every individual is in a position to protect themselves and their data online" when it is made by a government that can't even protect, as proven by events in May 2015, its own data against hacking attacks?

In November 2015, the Swiss director David Bernet's documentary *Democracy*, on the efforts toward a EU Data Protection Reform, was released. The subtitle (*Im Rausch der Daten*: High on data) points to the ambivalent, problematic relationship—if not love—our society has developed with big data. The film narrates the engagement of left-wing politicians and civil-rights activists in favor of severe data protection against their opponents: the business world and its lobbyists in Brussels. In December 2015, the European Parliament agreed on the proposed reform, enhancing the level of data protection for individuals via the threat of high fines for companies who fail to comply. The reform contains two interesting and important tools to ensure compliance with data-protection rules: "data-protection officers," who are to be appointed by public authorities and companies to overview risky data processing, and "impact assessment," which is to be conducted in order to avoid data processing, in particular when using new technology, that infringes on the rights and freedoms of individuals.[9] Such measures echo the proposal by Mayer-Schönberger and Cukier in their 2013 book *Big Data*: that "algorithmist" experts review big-data analyses in order to advise companies and protect consumers.[10] It is encouraging that such ideas are finding their way from academic texts into legal codes. The hope is, however, that the premise of the EU Data Protection Reform and Bernet's documentary remains true for the time being: that data protection and privacy are values that, in principle, prevail over the interests of promising business innovations and the seductions of increased comfort.

NOTES

PREFACE

1. http://nextconf.eu/nextII/nextII-means-data-love (no longer online; grammar issues in the original).

2. The terms "data" and "information" do not differ quantitatively, as is suggested when referring to a bit of data as a "piece of information," but qualitatively. Data (as givens or facts; *datum* in Latin) embody the lowest level in the chain of perception, preceding both information (as processed data; *informare* in Latin) and knowledge (as interconnected information or a "serial event of cooperation and collaboration," in the formulation of Manfred Faßler, *Der infogene Mensch. Entwurf einer Anthropologie* [Munich: Wilhelm Fink 2008], 281, stressing the processual character of knowledge). From the perspective of perception theory, however, it is questionable that data (as givens before interpretation and the construction of meaning) exist for the observer. As an alternative to "data," the suggestion has been made to use "capta" (from the English "to capture") in order to keep in one's mind the inevitable "taking" of the given. See Johanna Drucker, "Humanities Approaches to Graphical Display," *Digital Humanities Quarterly* 5, no. 1 (2011), http://www.digitalhumanities.org/dhq/5/1/000091/000091.html. This term, though, subverts the difference between data and information (as *processed* data). Since the purpose of this book is not a terminological discussion, it may suffice to keep in mind the indicated difference among data, information, and knowledge.

3. http://www.datalove.me; http://www.datalove.me/about.html.

1. INTELLIGENCE AGENCY LOGIC

1. *Welt am Sonntag* (July 28, 2013), http://www.welt.de/print/wams
   /article118447661/Steinbrueck-dankt-Edward-Snowden.html); Wort
   .lu (September 20, 2013), http://www.wort.lu/en/view/thank-you-mr
   -snowden-says-eu-s-reding-523bdfa4e4b0c159be9abbba.
2. *Huffington Post* (July 18, 2013), http://www.huffingtonpost.com/2013
   /07/18/jimmy-carter-edward-snowden_n_3616930.html.
3. *Der Spiegel* (July 27, 2013), http://www.spiegel.de/politik/deutschland
   /nsa-ex-innenminister-schily-haelt-furcht-vor-ueberwachung-fuer
   -paranoid-a-913507.html.

2. DOUBLE INDIFFERENCE

1. See the lecture by the political scientist Christoph Bieber, "Politik und
   Staat im Netz. Social Media nach dem NSA-Abhörskandal und der
   Wahl in Deutschland" (Politics and state on the net: Social media after
   the NSA phone tapping scandal and elections in Germany), one in the
   series *Digital Media Studies in der Praxis. Wie die Geisteswissenschaften
   auf die neuen Medien reagieren* (Practical digital media studies: How the
   humanities react to the new media), which I organized at Basel University on September 24, 2013. Gerhart Baum compares it to Fukushima
   in an article in the *Frankfurter Allgemeine Zeitung* (September 24, 2013),
   http://www.faz.net/aktuell/feuilleton/gastbeitrag-von-gerhart-baum
   -ich-will-dass-wir-beissen-koennen-12589869.html.
2. http://nikeplus.nike.com/plus/what_is_fuel.
3. Frank Schirrmacher, "Digitale Autonomie. Europa 3.0," *Frankfurter
   Allgemeine Zeitung* (July 4, 2013), http://www.faz.net/aktuell/feuilleton
   /digitale-autonomie-europa-3-0-12271068.html.
4. Chris Chesher, "Colonizing Virtual Reality: Construction of the Discourse of Virtual Reality, 1984–1992," *Cultronix* 1, no. 1 (1994), http://
   cultronix.eserver.org/chesher.

3. SELF-TRACKING AND SMART THINGS

1. Evgeny Morozov, "Information Consumerism: The Price of Hypocrisy," *Frankfurter Allgemeine Zeitung* (July 24, 2013), http://www.faz.net
   /aktuell/feuilleton/debatten/ueberwachung/information-consumerism
   -the-price-of-hypocrisy-12292374.html.

2. This is the introductory sentence on a website for tracking sleeping patterns. http://www.selftrackinghq.com/zeo.

3. This is a quote from a devoted self-tracker in Klint Finley's article "The Quantified Man: How an Obsolete Tech Guy Rebuilt Himself for the Future," *Wired* (February 22, 2012), http://www.wired.com/wiredenter prise/2013/02/quantified-work/all.

4. Zygmunt Bauman and David Lyon, *Liquid Surveillance: A Conversation* (Cambridge: Polity, 2013), 71. Bauman is referring to John Burnham's *The Managerial Revolution* (New York: John Day, 1941).

5. Gary Wolf, "Know Thyself: Tracking Every Facet of Life, from Sleep to Mood to Pain, 24/7/365," *Wired* (June 22, 2009), https://archive .wired.com/medtech/health/magazine/17-07/lbnp_knowthyself ?currentPage=all.

6. Jamin Brophy-Warren, "The New Examined Life: Why More People Are Spilling the Statistics of Their Lives on the Web," *Wall Street Journal* (December 6, 2008), http://online.wsj.com/article/SB122852285532784401 .html.

7. The first example was the subject of a discussion at the Quantified Self conference in 2011 in Mountain View, California. See Emily Singer's report on the conference, "'Self-Tracking' für ein besseres Leben" (Self-tracking for a better life), *Technology Review* (June 15, 2011), http://www .heise.de/tr/artikel/Self-Tracking-fuer-ein-besseres-Leben-1259259 .html. The second example was reported by Julia Friedrichs in her article "Das tollere Ich" (The super me) in the magazine of the weekly *Die Zeit* (August 8, 2013), http://www.zeit.de/2013/33 /selbstoptimierung-leistungssteigerung-apps.

8. Gary Wolf, one of their protagonists, underlines exactly this altruistic aspect of self-tracking: "Oddly, though, self-tracking culture is not particularly individualistic. In fact, there is a strong tendency among self-trackers to share data and collaborate on new ways of using it. People monitoring their diet using *Tweet What You Eat!* can take advantage of crowdsourced calorie counters; people following their baby's sleep pattern with *Trixie Tracker* can graph it against those of other children; women watching their menstrual cycle at *MyMonthlyCycles* can use online tools to match their chart with others'. The most ambitious sites are aggregating personal data for patient-driven drug trials and medical research. Self-trackers seem eager to contribute to our knowledge about human life." Wolf, "Know Thyself."

9. Helga Nowotny, "Wissenschaft neu denken. Vom verlässlichen Wissen zum gesellschaftlich robusten Wissen," in *Die Verfasstheit der Wissensgesellschaft*, ed. Karsten Gerlog and Anne Ulrich (Münster: Westfälisches Dampfboot, 2006), 27, 33.

10. See Morozov, "Information Consumerism."

4. ECOLOGICAL DATA DISASTER

1. Regarding this future project at the University of Newcastle, see "Smile, You're on BinCam! Five Households Agree to Let Snooping Device Record Everything They Throw Away," *Daily Mail* (March 4, 2011), http://www.dailymail.co.uk/news/article-2000566/Smile-Youre-bin -cam-The-snooping-device-record-throw-away.html.

2. Evgeny Morozov, "Information Consumerism: The Price of Hypocrisy," *Frankfurter Allgemeine Zeitung* (*FAZ*) (July 24, 2013), http://www .faz.net/aktuell/feuilleton/debatten/ueberwachung/information -consumerism-the-price-of-hypocrisy-12292374.html.

3. This example is reported, with reference to the German company Metro Group, by Andreas Weigend, former chief scientist at Amazon, in his talk "The Social Data Revolution: More Efficient Than the KGB?" at the World Innovation Forum, New York (May 8, 2010), http://fora.tv/2010/06 /08/Andreas_Wigend_Marketing_and_Web_20/The_Social _Data_Revolution_More_Efficient_than_the_KGB. Four years later, Apple's iBeacons sensor promised such "location-based marketing," possibly starting a trend, as it did with the iPhone.

4. Hans Jonas, *The Imperative of Responsibility* (Chicago: University of Chicago Press, 1984), 26. Originally published in German in 1979.

5. Morozov expands on this complexity in "The Real Privacy Problem," *MIT Technology Review* (October 22, 2013); and in his book *To Save Everything, Click Here: The Folly of Technological Solutionism* (New York: PublicAffairs, 2013).

6. Wolfgang Michal, "Überwachung und Verfassungsrecht. Die Kränkung der Demokraten," *Frankfurter Allgemeine Zeitung* (August 5, 2013), http://www.faz.net/aktuell/feuilleton/ueberwachung-und-verfassung -srecht-die-kraenkung-der-demokraten-12369328.html; Gerhart Baum, "Ich will, dass wir beißen können," *Frankfurter Allgemeine Zeitung* (September 24, 2013), http://www.faz.net/aktuell/feuilleton/gastbeitrag -von-gerhart-baum-ich-will-dass-wir-beissen-koennen-12589869 .html.

7. Frank Schirrmacher, "Politik im Datenzeitalter. Was die SPD verschläft," *Frankfurter Allgemeine Zeitung* (September 25, 2013), http://www.faz.net/aktuell/politik-im-datenzeitalter-was-die-spd-verschlaeft-12591683.html. See also Frank Schirrmacher on the Beckmann TV show *Der gläserne Bürger—ausgespäht und ausgeliefert* (July 18, 2013), minute 102.

8. The consensus between the views of the digital native Morozov (born 1994) and those of the digital immigrant Schirrmacher (born 1959) regarding the negative evaluation of today's developments in technology shows that cultural criticism or even pessimism cannot be attributed unproblematically to the older generation. Also Michel Serres (born 1930) shows with his book *Petite Poucette* (2012) that the older generation does not necessarily behave in a way that is motivated by cultural pessimism.

9. On this, see the paragraphs concerning Charles Fourier's social utopias, the glass architecture of the early twentieth century, surrealism, and Trotsky, in *Manfred Schneider. Transparenzraum* (Berlin: Matthes & Seitz, 2013).

10. Georg Simmel, *The Sociology of Georg Simmel*, trans. and ed. Kurt H. Wolf (New York: Macmillan, 1950), 330; Peter Handke, *Am Felsfenster morgens* (Salzburg, 1998), 336.

5. COLD CIVIL WAR

1. "Ist das Internet noch zu retten?" *Die Zeit Online* (August 8, 2013), http://www.zeit.de/digital/datenschutz/2013-08/internet-pioniere-nsa.

2. On the demand for transparency, see Tal Zarsky, "Mining the Networked Self," *Jerusalem Review of Legal Studies* 6, no. 1 (2012): 120–136; Tal Zarsky, "Transparent Predictions," *University of Illinois Law Review* 4 (2013): 1503–1569.

3. Gilles Deleuze, "Post-Scriptum on the Societies of Control," *October* 59 (Winter 1992): 6. https://sites.google.com/site/deleuzemedia/textes/post-scriptum-sur-les-societes-de-controle.

4. Jürgen Habermas, "Technology and Science as Ideology," in *Towards a Rational Society: Student Protest, Science, and Politics*, trans. Jeremy Shapiro (Boston: Beacon, 1979), 107.

5. Ibid., 106.

6. Zygmunt Bauman and David Lyon, *Liquid Surveillance: A Conversation* (Cambridge: Polity, 2013), 86. See Klint Finley, "The Quantified Man:

How an Obsolete Tech Guy Rebuilt Himself for the Future," *Wired* (February 22, 2012), http://www.wired.com/wiredenterprise/2013/02/quantified-work/all.

7. Hans Jonas, *The Imperative of Responsibility* (Chicago: University of Chicago Press, 1984), 26.

8. Ellen Ullman, *Close to the Machine: Technophilia and Its Discontents* (New York, 2012), 98, 91. Anna North presents these quotes in her article "When Technology Makes Work Worse," *New York Times* (August 19, 2014). North also refers to Rhodri Marsden's text "Is Your Boss Spying on You?" *Independent* (March 19, 2014). Marsden concludes that the results of such analyses "could eventually produce data sets that cover the entire career of an individual, following us from job to job and depriving us of the opportunity to creatively airbrush our past within the context of a one-page CV." http://www.independent.co.uk/life-style/gadgets-and-tech/features/is-your-boss-spying-on-you-9203169.html. From a management perspective the transparent employee is desirable exactly for the reason that it prevents such airbrushing. The morals—this is the paradoxical and absurd aspect of such analyses—are on the side of those who want to reveal, not to conceal, the truth. For Evolv's self-description, see www.linkedin.com/company/evolv-on-demand.

9. The first quote is by David Lyon in Finley, "The Quantified Man"; the second quote is by Zygmunt Baumann in Baumann and Lyon, *Liquid Surveillance*, 168, 130.

10. See Iljia Trojanow, "Die Kollateralschäden des kalten Bürgerkriegs," *Neue Zürcher Zeitung* (August 2, 2013), http://www.nzz.ch/meinung/uebersicht/die-kollateralschaeden-des-kalten-buergerkriegs-1.18126416.

11. "Control and Becoming" (Gilles Deleuze in conversation with Antonio Negri), http://www.uib.no/sites/w3.uib.no/files/attachments/6._deleuze-control_and_ becoming.pdf. Gilles Deleuze, *Negotiations, 1972–1990* (New York: Columbia University Press, 1995), 175.

6. DATA-MINING BUSINESS

1. For details concerning the calculation, see http://klout.com/corp/klout_score.

2. Alfred W. Crosby, *The Measure of Reality: Quantification and Western Society* (Cambridge: Cambridge University Press, 1997).

3. Thomas H. Davenport and D. J. Patil, "Data Scientist: The Sexiest Job of the 21st Century," *Harvard Business Review* (October 2012), http://hbr.org/2012/10/data-scientist-the-sexiest-job-of-the-21st-century; Ian Ayre, *Super Crunchers: Why Thinking-by-Numbers Is the New Way to Be Smart* (New York: Bantam, 2008).

4. On the job sharing of data mining, see Viktor Meyer-Schönberger and Kenneth Cukier, *Big Data: A Revolution That Will Transform How We Live, Work, and Think* (New York: Houghton Mifflin Harcourt, 2013), chap. 7.

5. Ibid., 3–5.

7. SOCIAL ENGINEERS WITHOUT A CAUSE

1. http://www.youtube.com/watch?v=boM3EAuz-oU; http://www.hapilabs.com/products-hapifork.asp.

2. http://summly.com/publishers.html.

3. It is in exactly this framework of customization that Viktor Meyer-Schönberger and Kenneth Cukier are surprised that Amazon does not sell its data on the reading habits of its Kindle users to authors and publishers: "For authors a feedback would be also useful; they would be able to track when the reader stops reading the book and they could then improve their texts." Viktor Meyer-Schönberger and Kenneth Cukier, *Big Data: A Revolution That Will Transform How We Live, Work, and Think* (New York: Houghton Mifflin Harcourt, 2013), 167.

4. For a recent appeal to save the book as means of reflection and imagination against the practice of "developing written material to suit sales strategies," see Ursula K. Le Guin's acceptance speech at the National Book Awards on November 20, 2014.

5. William Shakespeare, *Hamlet*, 3.1. A good example of how little tinkerers allowed their enterprises to be "sicklied" by thought is given by Todd Humphrey, the director of the University of Texas at Austin's Radionavigation Laboratory, in his TED talk "How to Fool a GPS" in February 2012, while promoting equipping all objects with GPS-"dots": "I couldn't find my shoes one recent morning. And as usual I had to ask my wife if she had seen them. But I shouldn't have to bother my wife with this kind of triviality. I should be able to ask my house where my shoes are." http://www.ted.com/talks/todd_humphreys_how_to _fool_a_gps. The joke received the laughter hoped for in the TED talk

and leaves little room for this troublesome objection: how much better it is to have to ask one's wife than to risk that others, whom the wife would never answer, could ask the house as well.

6. In his book *The Cultural Logic of Computation* (Cambridge, Mass.: Harvard University Press, 2009), David Golumbia criticizes "computationalism as the belief in the power of computation, as commitment to the view that a great deal, perhaps all, of human and social experience can be explained via computational processes" (8). Evgeny Morozov varies this criticism in his book *The Net Delusion: The Dark Side of Internet Freedom* (New York: PublicAffairs, 2011), with the key terms "internet-centrism" and "cyber-utopianism" representing the conviction that all social problems can be and should be solved through the Internet (xv). Later, in his book *To Save Everything, Click Here: The Folly of Technological Solutionism* (New York: PublicAffairs, 2013), Morozov reinforces his critique under the key word "solutionism." The "softwarization of society" is, among others, discussed by David M. Berry in his *Critical Theory and the Digital* (New York: Bloomsbury, 2014), where Berry notes a "transition from a rational juridical epistemology to an *authoritarian-computational* epistemology" and points out the presence of software engineers within their products: "their rationalities, expressed through particular logics, embedded in the interface and the code, become internalized within the user as a particular habitus, or way of doing, appropriate to certain social activities" (12, 38).

8. SILENT REVOLUTION

1. Rick Smolan and Jennifer Erwitt, eds., *The Human Face of Big Data* (New York: Sterling, 2013), 19.
2. Eric Schmidt and Jared Cohen, *The New Digital Age: Transforming Nations, Businesses, and Our Lives* (New York: Vintage, 2014), 4ff.
3. Ibid., 57.
4. Ibid., 34.
5. Morozov offers this term in his book *The Net Delusion: The Dark Side of Internet Freedom* (New York: PublicAffairs, 2011), with respect to the media euphoria of the Arab spring in 2009, which generated such headlines as "Facebook Revolution" and "In Egypt, Twitter Trumps Torture."
6. Schmidt and Cohen, *The New Digital Age*, 66.

7. Hans Jonas, *The Imperative of Responsibility* (Chicago: University of Chicago Press, 1984), 67, 63.

8. Sherry Turkle, *Alone Together: Why We Expect More from Technology and Less from Each Other* (New York: Basic Books, 2011); Viktor Mayer-Schönberger, *Delete: The Virtue of Forgetting in the Digital Age* (Princeton, N.J.: Princeton University Press, 2009); Nicholas Carr, *The Shallows—What the Internet Is Doing to Our Brains* (New York: Norton, 2010).

9. Gary T. Marx, "An Ethics for the New Surveillance," *Information Society* 14, no. 3 (1998): 171–185; Alex Pentland, "Reality Mining of Mobile Communications: Toward a New Deal on Data," in *The Global Information Technology Report 2008–2009*, ed. Soumitra Dutta and Irene Mia, http://hd.media.mit.edu/wef_globalit.pdf. Of course, the privacy debate demands clearing up who owns the data both technologically (is it the individual who produces its geodata, or is it the provider?) and socially (living in an apartment building, how much privacy can the individual demand from Google Maps?).

9. ALGORITHMS

1. On the problems of terminology, see, for example, Peter Wegener, "Why Interaction Is More Powerful Than Algorithms," *Communications of the ACM* 40, no. 5 (1997): 80–91; Moshe Y. Vardi, "What Is an Algorithm?" *Communications of the ACM* 55, no. 3 (2012): 5. Moreover, computer sciences differentiate functionally between many different algorithms: searching, sorting, classification, and optimizing algorithms as dynamic, evolutionary, or probabilistic algorithms, as cryptographic, epidemic, or ant-colony optimization algorithms. For an extended discussion of the algorithm, see Thomas H. Cormen, Charles E. Leiserson, and Ronald L. Rivest, *Introduction to Algorithms* (Cambridge, Mass.: MIT Press, 2009); Mikhail J. Atallah and Marina Blanton, eds., *Algorithms and Theory of Computation Handbook* (Boca Raton, Fla.: Chapman & Hall, 2009). See also the *Dictionary of Algorithms and Data Structures*, http://xlinux.nist.gov/dads; and Robert Kowalski's essay "Algorithm = Logic + Control," *Communications of the ACM* 22, no. 7 (July 1979): 424–436. My thanks go to Marcus Burkhardt for his references to the discussions in the field (*Digitale Datenbanken: Eine Medientheorie im Zeitalter von Big Data* [Bielefeld: transcript, 2015]).

2. Andrew Goffrey, "Algorithm," in *Software Studies: A Lexicon*, ed. Matthew Fuller (Cambridge, Mass.: MIT Press, 2008), 19.

3. Eli Pariser, *Filter Bubble: How the New Personalized Web Is Changing What We Read and How We Think* (New York: Penguin, 2011), 15.

4. Berthold Brecht, *Stories of Mr. Keuner*, trans. Martin Chalmers (San Francisco: City Lights, 2001), 20.

5. Lada Adamic and Natalie Glance, "The Political Blogosphere and the 2004 Election: Divided They Blog," in *Proceedings of the 3rd International Workshop on Link Discovery* (New York, 2005), 36–43. See also Cass Sunstein, *Infotopia: How Many Minds Produce Knowledge* (Oxford: Oxford University Press, 2008). On the term "Daily Me," see Cass Sunstein, *Republic.com* (Princeton, N.J.: Princeton University Press, 2001).

6. See Andrew Shapiro, *Control Revolution* (New York: PublicAffairs, 1999); Gordon Graham, *The Internet: A Philosophical Inquiry* (1999); Sunstein, *Republic.com*. The psychological explanation for the human interest in the filter bubble was already given in Leon Festinger's *Theory of Cognitive Dissonance* (Stanford, Calif.: Stanford University Press, 1957), and the necessity of encountering otherness and contradictoriness is discussed by Ernesto Laclau's *Emancipation(s)* (New York: Verso, 1996).

7. David Lazer, Alex Pentland, et al., "Computational Social Science," *Social Science* 323 (February 6, 2009): 721–723.

8. This is how the enthusiasm for this form of electronic shackles in service of the organizational sciences sounds in the original: "Face-to-face group interactions could be assessed over time with 'sociometers.' Such electronic devices could be worn to capture physical proximity, location, movement, and other facets of individual behavior and collective interactions. The data could raise interesting questions about, for example, patterns of proximity and communication within an organization, and flow patterns associated with high individual and group performance." Ibid., 722.

9. See Cass R. Sunstein, "It's for Your Own Good!" *New York Review of Books* (March 7, 2013), http://www.nybooks.com/articles/archives/2013/mar/07/its-your-own-good. Sunstein is referring to Sarah Conly's book *Against Autonomy: Justifying Coercive Paternalism* (2013) that, given the weight problems, the debts, and the lack of social security of aging American citizens, pleads for the intervention of the state into its citizens' freedom to make decisions on their own.

10. See Theodor W. Adorno, "Sociology and Empirical Research," in *The Positivist Dispute in German Sociology*, trans. Glyn Adey and David Frisby (London: Heinemann, 1976). On the algorithm as a victory of Leibniz's logical syllogisms over Voltaire's critical rationalism, see David Golumbia, *The Cultural Logic of Computation* (Cambridge, Mass.: Harvard University Press, 2009), 189–196. On the criticism of the formalist model of rationality, see Hilary Putnam, *Reason, Truth, and History* (Cambridge: Cambridge University Press, 1981).

11. In the chapter "The Perils of Algorithmic Gatekeeping" in Morozov's book *To Save Everything, Click Here: The Folly of Technological Solutionism* (New York: PublicAffairs, 2013), he further illustrates the absurdity and danger of human freedom of opinion when algorithms pass judgment on certain key terms within the contents of journalist articles, with the consequence of excommunicating these articles from the Google cosmos.

12. https://ifttt.com/recipes/49639; https://ifttt.com/recipes/62433; https://ifttt.com/recipes/129817.

13. See Bill Wasik, "In the Programmable World, All Our Objects Will Act as One," *Wired* 21, no. 6 (May 14, 2013), http://www.wired.com/gadgetlab/2013/05/internet-of-things/all.

10. ABSENCE OF THEORY

1. *Wired* (June 23, 2008), http://www.wired.com/science/discoveries/magazine/16-07/pb_theory.

2. Hans Jörg Rheinberger, "Wie werden aus Spuren Daten, und wie verhalten sich Daten zu Fakten?" in *Nach Feierabend 2007: Daten; Züricher Jahrbuch für Wissensgeschichte*, ed. David Gugerli et al. (Berlin: Diaphanes, 2007), 3:123–124: "Currently data only make sense and only acquire meaning if they are accessible in a structured way. In this context there has been talk about a true epistemological revolution taking place at this moment. The argument is that a transition from research based on hypotheses to one based on data has taken place. I.e., traces are no longer generated through phenomena but pooled as data in order to bring yet unknown, new facts to light."

3. See Timothy Lenoir, one of the prominent representatives in digital humanities in 2008 in an e-mail to N. Katherine Hayles. N. Katherine Hayles, *How We Think: Digital Media and Contemporary Technogenesis*

(Chicago: University of Chicago Press, 2012), 33. See also Patricia Cohen, "Humanities 2.0. Digital Keys for Unlocking the Humanities' Riches," *New York Times* (November 16, 2010).

4. David M. Berry, "The Computational Turn: Thinking About the Digital Humanities," *Culture Machine* 12 (2011): 4.

5. Viktor Meyer-Schönberger and Kenneth Cukier, *Big Data: A Revolution That Will Transform How We Live, Work, and Think* (New York: Houghton Mifflin Harcourt, 2013), 87–88. On the paradigm change in the sciences, see Alfred Nordmann, Hans Radder, and Gregor Schiemann, eds., *Science Transformed? Debating Claims of an Epochal Break* (Pittsburgh, Penn.: University of Pittsburgh Press, 2011).

6. Brian Eno on October 29, 2009, in the blog of the magazine *Prospect*. http://www.prospectmagazine.co.uk/blog/the-post-theoretical-age /#.UkSPYYKEO2w.

7. Pierre Nora, "Between Memory and History. Les Lieux de Memoire," *Representations* 26, special issue: *Memory and Counter-Memory* (Spring 1989): 8.

8. Jean-François Lyotard, "The Sublime and the Avant-Garde," in *The Lyotard Reader*, ed. Andrew Benjamin (Malden, Mass.: Blackwell, 1991), 196–211; Erika Fischer-Lichte, *The Transformative Power of Performance: A New Aesthetics*, trans. Saskia Iris Jain (New York: Routledge, 2008); Hans Ulrich Gumbrecht, *The Production of Presence: What Meaning Cannot Convey* (Stanford, Calif.: Stanford University Press, 2003). For an extensive discussion of these aesthetics on the background of the postmodern condition and digital media see Roberto Simanowski, *Digital Art and Meaning: Reading Kinetic Poetry, Text Machines, Mapping Art, and Interactive Installations* (Minneapolis: University of Minnesota Press, 2011), 1–26.

9. Jean-François Lyotard, "Newman: The Instant," in *The Inhuman: Reflections on Time*, trans. Geoffrey Bennington and Rachel Bowlby (Cambridge: Polity, 1991), 88.

10. Hans Ulrich Gumbrecht, *Production of Presence: What Meaning Cannot Convey* (Stanford, Calif.: Stanford University Press, 2004), 19, 146.

11. Jacques Rancière, *Aesthetics and Its Discontents* (Cambridge: Polity, 2009), 105, 104.

12. Norbert Bolz, "Theorie der Müdigkeit—Theoriemüdigkeit," *telepolis* 3 (September 1997): 43.

13. Jean-François Lyotard, "Apostil on Narratives," in *The Postmodern Explained: Correspondence, 1982–1985* (Minneapolis: University of Minnesota Press, 1997), 18, 19.

11. COMPULSIVE MEASURING

1. http://blog.facebook.com/blog.php?post=387623222130.
2. Sophie Crocoll, "Twitter weiß es besser," *Die Zeit* (June 6, 2012), http://www.zeit.de/2012/24/F-Soziale-Netzwerke.
3. With this expectation the Swiss Next Generation Finance Invest AG justifies its engagement with StockPulse, a startup of two IT business engineers from Cologne that follows communications on financial markets in the realm of social media and analyzes up to one hundred thousand content items daily in order to predict volatility and price movements with trading signals for stocks, currency, and raw material. *Half-Annual Report* (August 21, 2012), http://blog.nextgfi.com/page/3. Page no longer accessible.
4. Richard Münch, *Akademischer Kapitalismus. Über die politische Ökonomie der Hochschulreform* (Frankfurt am Main: Suhrkamp, 2011), 13. See Theodor M. Porter, *Trust in Numbers: The Pursuit of Objectivity in Science and Public Life* (Princeton, N.J.: Princeton University Press, 1995).

12. THE PHENOMENOLOGY OF THE NUMERABLE

1. See the study "Facebook-Nutzung macht neidisch und unzufrieden" (Facebook use makes you jealous and dissatisfied) at Humboldt University, Berlin and Technical University, Darmstadt, on six hundred Facebook users. http://www.hu-berlin.de/pr/pressemitteilungen/pm1301/pm_130121_00.
2. In the words of the Jawbone product development engineering manager Travis Bogard: "The number one correlate with your weight is what your friends are doing." http://www.fastcodesign.com/1665351/jawbone-releases-up-a-wristband-for-tracking-your-wellness.
3. The British supermarket chain Tesco is checking the productivity of their employees using such bracelets, arguing that this facilitates their work logistically. *The Independent* (February 13, 2013), http://www.independent.co.uk/news/business/news/tesco-accused-of-using-electronic-armbands-to-monitor-its-staff-8493952.html

4. Byung-Chul Han, *Digitale Rationalität und das Ende des kommunikativen Handelns* (Berlin: Matthes & Seitz, 2013), 33, 20ff. On the discussion of the jury theorem in Nicolas de Condorcet's *Essai sur l'application de l'analyse à la probabilité des décisions rendues à la pluralité des voix* (1785) and his relationship to democracy, see Cass R. Sunstein, *Infotopia: How Many Minds Produce Knowledge* (Oxford: Oxford University Press, 2006), chaps. 1–2.

5. The same removal of protection by the experts occurs in academia, where unprofitable but important programs can no longer be backed up by the faculty of a department if each program reports directly and independently to the financial office.

6. Jürgen Mittelstrass, "Bildung und ethische Masse," in *Die Zukunft der Bildung*, ed. Nelson Kilius, Jürgen Kluge, and Linda Reisch (Frankfurt am Main: Suhrkamp, 2002), 257.

7. Ulrich Beck, *Risk Society: Towards a New Modernity* (London: Sage, 1992), 157, 167.

8. http://hedonometer.org/about.html.

9. On the terminological index on May 2, 2011, see http://www.hedonometer.org/wordshift.html?date=2011-05-02; on happiness ranking, see http://hedonometer.org/words.html. The ranking list on Hedonometer is based on processing through Amazon's Mechanical Turk, in the course of which the predefined words are given a value between 1 and 9, although ethnic, cultural, gender, age, and educational composition were completely unaccounted for.

10. Michel Callon and John Law, "On Qualculation, Agency, and Otherness," *Environment and Planning* 23 (2005): 717–733.

11. William H. Starbuck, "How Much Better Are the Most Prestigious Journals? The Statistics of Academic Publication," *Organization Science* 16 (2005): 180–200; Alfred Kieser, "JOURQUAL—der Gebrauch, nicht der Missbrauch, ist das Problem. Oder: Warum Wirtschaftsinformatik die beste deutschsprachige betriebswirtschaftliche Zeitschrift ist," *Die Betriebswirtschaft* 72 (2012): 93–110.

13. DIGITAL HUMANITIES

1. Marc Parry, "The Humanities Go Google," *Chronicle of Higher Education, Technology* 28 (May 2010), http://chronicle.com/article/The-Humanities-Go-Google/65713.

2. Franco Moretti, "Conjectures on World Literature," *New Left Review* 1 (2000): 57.

3. See the panel "The Dark Side of the Digital Humanities" at the MLA Convention in January 2013 and the lecture by Alan Liu, "Where Is Cultural Criticism in the Digital Humanities?" at the MLA Convention in January 2011.

4. http://nanopub.org/wordpress/?page_id=65; see Paul Groth, Andrew Gibson, and Johannes Velterop, "The Anatomy of a Nanopublication," *Information Services and Use* 30, no. 1 (2010): 51–56. http://www.w3.org/wiki/images/c/co/HCLSIG$$SWANSIOC$$Actions$$Rhetor icalStructure$$meetings$$20100215$cwa-anatomy-nanopub-v3.pdf. The authors differentiate between concept ("smallest, unambiguous unit of thought"), triple ("a tuple of three concepts (subject, predicate, object)"), statement ("triple that is uniquely identifiable"), and annotation ("triple such that the subject of the triple is a statement") and define the nano-publication as: "A set of annotations that refer to the same statement and contains a minimum set of (community) agreed upon annotations."

5. Tripel means 3-tupel; tupel is a term for the synopsis of an ordered list of mathematical objects sensitive to sequence.

6. "The Semantic Web is, bluntly said, nothing else but technocratic neo-scholasticism based on a naive if not dangerous belief that the world can be described according to a single and universally valid viewpoint; in other words, a blatant example of cybernetic control ideology and engineering blindness to ambiguity and cultural issues." Florian Cra-mer, "Animals That Belong to the Emperor: Failing Universal Classifi-cation Schemes from Aristotle to the Semantic Web," *Nettime* 29 (September 2007), http://www.nettime.org/Lists-Archives/nettime-l-0712/msg00043.html. "Any attempt at a global ontology is doomed to fail, because meta-data describes a worldview." Clay Shirky, "The Seman-tic Web, Syllogism, and Worldview" (November 7, 2003), http://www.shirky.com/writings/herecomeseverybody/semantic_syllogism.html. I would like to thank Marcus Burkhardt for drawing my attention to this discussion in his dissertation *Medium/Computer/Datenbank. Ansätze einer medientheoretischen Grundlegung*, University of Giessen (Spring 2014). On the discussion of this example and the epistemological prob-lems of the semantic web, see Burkhardt, *Medium*, 276–290.

7. Grigoris Antoniou and Frank van Harmelen, *A Semantic Web Primer* (Cambridge, Mass.: MIT Press, 2008), 246–247: "The motto of the

Semantic Web is not the enforcement of a single ontology but rather 'let a thousand ontologies blossom.'"

8. Antoniou and van Harmelen themselves point out this aspect of invisibility without relating it to the promise of the polyphony of ontologies: "Navigation or personalization engines can be powered by underlying ontologies, expressed in RDF Schema or OWL, without users ever being confronted with the ontologies, let alone their representation languages" (ibid., 247).

9. Niels-Oliver Walkowski, "Text, Denken und E-Science. Eine internationale Annäherung an eine Konstellation," *Nach Feierabend. Zürcher Jahrbuch für Wissensgeschichte* 9: *Digital Humanities* (Diaphanes, 2013), 45–46. See also Richard Sennett's distinction, with respect to the logic of collaboration software such as GoogleWave, between information sharing as "an exercise in definition and precision" and communication which "is as much about what is left unsaid as said" and "mines the realm of suggestions and connotation." Richard Sennett, *Together: The Rituals, Pleasures, and Politics of Cooperation* (New York: Penguin, 2012), 28.

10. Theodor Adorno, "The Essay as Form," in *Notes to Literature* (New York: Columbia University Press, 1991), 1:9.

11. Ibid., 1:12, 1:18.

12. Ibid., 1:13, 1:16–17.

13. Stephen Ramsay, "The Hermeneutics of Screwing Around; or What You Do with a Million Books," lecture at Brown University (2010). See Ramsay's article "Toward an Algorithmic Criticism," *Literary and Linguistic Computing* 18, no. 2 (2003): 167–174, which conceives of algorithmic analysis not as verification of interpretations but as inspiration for hermeneutic attempts quite in the style of art reception.

14. George P. Landow, *Hypertext 2.0: The Convergence of Contemporary Critical Theory and Technology* (Baltimore, Md.: Johns Hopkins University Press, 1997), 82.

15. Terence Harpold, "Conclusions," in *Hyper/Text/Theorie*, ed. George P. Landow (Baltimore, Md.: Johns Hopkins University Press, 1994), 189–222; David Kolb, "Socrates in the Labyrinth," in *Hyper/Text/Theorie*, ed. George P. Landow (Baltimore, Md.: Johns Hopkins University Press, 1994), 323–344.

16. Anne Burdick, Johanna Drucker, Peter Lunenfeld, Todd Presner, and Jeffrey Schnapp, *Digital_Humanities* (Cambridge, Mass.: MIT Press 2012), 10.

14. LESSING'S REJOINDER

1. Lev Manovich, *The Language of New Media* (Cambridge, Mass.: MIT Press, 2001), 225.
2. David M. Berry, "The Computational Turn: Thinking About the Digital Humanities," *Culture Machine* 12 (2011): 7, with a quote from Bill Readings' *The University in Ruins* (Cambridge, Mass.: Harvard University Press, 1996), 66: "That is the point of the pedagogy of *Bildung*, which teaches knowledge acquisition as a *process* rather than the acquisition of knowledge as a *product*."
3. Ibid., 10.
4. Sabine Maasen, *Wissenssoziologie* (Bielefeld: transcript, 2009), 86.
5. Gotthold Ephraim Lessing, *A Rejoinder*, in *Philosophical and Theological Writings*, ed. H. B. Nisbet (Cambridge: Cambridge University Press, 2005), 98.
6. Ibid.
7. Hannah Arendt, *Men in Dark Times* (San Diego, Calif.: Harcourt, Brace, 1968), 27ff.
8. Ibid., 10.
9. Ibid., 8.
10. Richard Rorty, *Philosophy and the Mirror of Nature* (Princeton, N.J.: Princeton University Press, 1979), 377. Claus Leggewie sees Rorty's reference to Lessing's endlessly deferring conception of truth as an expression of postmodern acceptance of difference and connects this philosophical position with the pragmatic problem of multiculturalism in his book *Multi kulti. Spielregeln für die Vielvölkerrepublik* (Berlin: Rotbuch, 1990), 134.
11. David Weinberger, "Die Digitale Glaskugel," in *Big Data. Das neue Versprechen des Allwissenheit*, ed. Heinrich Geiselberger and Tobias Moorstedt (Berlin: Suhrkamp, 2013), 236–237.
12. With a view to the terminological differentiation made at the outset, it becomes questionable whether, in strict terms, we can still use the category "knowledge" (or "understanding") here as "program of a deliberated insight or conception of recognition and delineation" or whether we should rather talk of information. Manfred Faßler, *Der infogene Mensch. Entwurf einer Anthropologie* (Munich: Wilhelm Fink, 2008), 277. Reconstructing the cognitive process that a book or an article makes possible as a structured processing of information will, at any rate, get lost in the course of shortening into selected excerpts or to the result of that process.

13. Weinberger, "Die Digitale Glaskugel," 236.
14. Ziauddin Sardar, "Alt.Civilizations. FAQ. Cyberspace as the Darker Side of the West," in *The Cybercultures Reader*, ed. David Bell and Barbara M. Kennedy (London: Routledge, 2000), 742.
15. Elena Esposito, *Soziales Vergessen: Formen und Medien des Gedächtnisses der Gesellschaft* (Frankfurt am Main: Suhrkamp, 2002), 318.
16. In my book *Facebook-Gesellschaft* (Matthes & Seitz, 2016), I take up this discussion from the perspective of narrative and memory theory.

15. GOD'S EYE

1. Zygmunt Bauman and David Lyon, *Liquid Surveillance: A Conversation* (Cambridge: Polity, 2013), 73, 59.
2. Didier Bigo, "Globalized (in)Security: The Field and the Ban-opticon," in *Translation, Biopolitics, Colonial Difference*, ed. Naoki Sakai and John Solomos, Traces: A Multilingual Series of Cultural Theory 4 (Hong Kong: Hong Kong University Press, 2006), 109–156; Thomas Mathiesen, "The Viewer Society: Michel Foucault's Panopticon Revisited," *Theoretical Criminology* 1, no. 2 (May 1997): 215–234.
3. Oscar Gandy, *The Panoptic Sort: A Political Economy of Personal Information* (Boulder, Colo.: Westview, 1993).
4. Holman W. Jenkins Jr., "Google and the Search for the Future," *Wall Street Journal* (August 14, 2010). The "anticipatory software" Google Now, launched in 2012, fulfills the goal specified for it at least to the extent that it indicates flight delays on its own because it knows the travel plans of its users from their Gmail-hosted e-mails.
5. Interview with Maria Bartiromo on CNBC (December 3, 2009), http://www.huffingtonpost.com/2009/12/07/google-ceo-on-priv acy-if_n_383105.html; interview with James Bennet (*The Atlantic*) at the Second Annual Washington Ideas Forum (October 2, 2010), http://www.theatlantic.com/technology/archive/2010/10/googles -ceo-the-laws-are-written-by-lobbyists/63908.
6. The inspiration—and the payback—for this commercial is of course the Super Bowl commercial by Pepsi-Cola from 1996 in which a surveillance camera shows how a Coca-Cola distributor in a supermarket steals a Pepsi can from the fridge. Here it is not the function of the surveillance camera that is given new meaning; it is the judgment of the convicted culprit, who in the logic of advertisement actually does

"the right thing." The twinkle in the eye is even implemented on the audio level. However, against the voluble enthusiasms of Coca-Cola, which are free of irony, it is to be feared that Pepsi's gesture hardly has a chance. http://www.youtube.com/watch?v=_cJzTgFPj64.

16. DATA HACKS

1. The concept of media literacy oriented by cultural studies and going beyond the bounds of merely functional knowledge is illustrated in the collection of essays coedited by the author: "Grundlagen der Medienbildung. Szenarien und Potentiale" (Basics of media education: scenarios and potentials), *dichtung-digital. A journal of art and culture in digital media* 43 (2014): http://www.dichtung-digital.de/en/journal/archiv/?issue=43. I take up the discussion of media literacy in my book *Medienbildung* (forthcoming with Matthes & Seitz in 2017).
2. http://skli.se/2012/10/14/i-like-what-i-see; http://adnauseam.io.
3. Ulises Ali Mejias, in his book *Off the Network: Disrupting the Digital World* (Minneapolis: University of Minnesota Press, 2013), calls this communication outside of the realms of control or capitalization by global social networks (the nodes of the Internet) "paranodal." Already Gilles Deleuze had invoked "hijack speech" in his interview with Antonio Negri entitled "Control and Becoming." http://www.uib.no/sites/w3.uib.no/files/attachments/6._deleuze-control_and_becoming.pdf. Gilles Deleuze, *Negotiations, 1972–1990* (New York: Columbia University Press, 1995), 175: "The key thing may be to create vacuoles of noncommunication, circuit breakers, so we can elude control." See Gilles Deleuze, "Post-Scriptum on the Societies of Control," *October* 59 (Winter 1992): 6. Referring to this passage in its manifesto *The Cybernetic Hypothesis* (2001), the French authors' collective Tiqqun calls for the creation of "opacity zones," the opening of "cavities, empty intervals, '*black blocs*' within the cybernetic matrix of power." http://theanarchistlibrary.org/library/tiqqun-the-cybernetic-hypothesis.
4. Jennifer Golbeck, "The Curly Fry Conundrum: Why Social Media 'Likes' Say More Than You Might Think," TED Talk (October 2013), minute 8:07–8:17, http://www.ted.com/talks/jennifer_golbeck_the_curly_fry_conundrum_why_social_media_likes_say_more_than_you_might_think#t-485502.

5. Vilém Flusser, *Does Writing Have a Future?* (Minneapolis: University of Minnesota Press, 2011).

6. The term "optical unconscious" is used by Walter Benjamin to indicate the fact that the technical image captures details that may otherwise— for example, if a scene is in process—be invisible to or overlooked by the human eye.

7. Viktor Meyer-Schönberger and Kenneth Cukier, *Big Data: A Revolution That Will Transform How We Live, Work, and Think* (New York: Houghton Mifflin Harcourt, 2013), 180.

8. Ibid., 182.

9. Ralph Haupter, "Unternehmerische Verantwortung im Zeitalter von Cloud Computing," in *Der digitale Dämon: Informations- und Kommunikationstechnologien zwischen Alltag und Ängsten*, ed. Ralph Haupter (München: Redline 2013).

17. ON THE RIGHT LIFE IN THE WRONG ONE

1. Norbert Bolz, *Die Konformisten des Andersseins. Ende der Kritik* (München: Fink 1999), 127 (German: "[der] schöne Traum von einer schlechten Welt").

2. Jacques Rancière, *Aesthetics and Its Discontents* (Cambridge: Polity, 2009), 104–105.

3. Norbert Bolz, *Das konsumistische Manifest* (München: Fink, 2002), 14, 16.

4. http://www.theguardian.com/commentisfree/2014/mar/11/snowden-nsa -fire-sxsw-silicon-valley-security.

5. TED interview, Charlie Rose and Larry Page (March 2014), "Where's Google Going Next?" http://www.ted.com/talks/larry_page_where_s _google_going_next. The critical questions that are not asked by Rose are all the more clearly revealed in a reading of Julian Assange, who sees the privacy problem in particular in Google's attempt to gain total control over information. "The Banality of 'Don't Be Evil,'" *New York Times* (June 1, 2013).

6. A site exemplifying the contradictions of this engagement was the Berlin conference on digital culture *re:publica* 2014, where even after fierce claims for more data privacy, advocates for the Internet of things were nonetheless given hardly any critical questions concerning the accumulation of private data. The problem is that people fail to see the link

between Snowden and the smart shower (which collects data about your habits while mapping your water usage). See Yvonne Hofstetter's gloomy lecture "Big Data? Intelligente Maschinen!" (Big data? intelligent machines!), https://re-publica.de/file/republica-2014-yvonne -hofstetter-big-data-intelligente-maschinen, on the one hand, and, on the other, Martin Vesper's good-humored product announcement "Wenn der Kühlschrank twittert: Das Zusammenspiel von Haushaltsgeräten in unserer vernetzten Welt" (When the refrigerator twitters: The interaction with domestic appliances in our networked world), https:// re-publica.de/file/republica-2014-martin-vesper-wenn-kuehlschrank-t.

7. Hans Jonas, *The Imperative of Responsibility* (Chicago: University of Chicago Press, 1984), 218.

EPILOGUE

1. Martin Schulz, "Technologischer Totalitarismus: Warum wir jetzt kämpfen müssen," *Frankfurter Allgemeine Zeitung* (February 16, 2014), http:// www.faz.net/aktuell/feuilleton/debatten/techno logischer-totalitarismus -warum-wir-jetzt-kaempfen-muessen-12786805.html; Gerhardt Baum, "Auf dem Weg zum Weltüberwachungsmarkt," *Frankfurter Allgemeine Zeitung* (February 20, 2014), http://www.faz.net/aktuell/feuilleton /debatten/die-digital-debatte/politik-in-der-digitalen-welt/gerhart -baum-antwortet-auf-martin-schulz-auf-dem-weg-zum-weltueberwac hungsmarkt-12810430.html; Christian Lindner, "Warum Europa digitale Autonomie braucht," *Frankfurter Allgemeine Zeitung* (March 6, 2014), http://www.faz.net/aktuell/ feuilleton/debatten/die-digital-debatte/politik -in-der-digitalen-welt/it-kapitalimus-fdp-chef-lindner-fuer-digitale -autonomie-europas-12833286.html; Sigmar Gabriel, "Unsere politischen Konsequenzen aus der Google-Debatte," *Frankfurter Allgemeine Zeitung* (May 16, 2014), http://www.faz.net/aktuell/feuilleton/debatten/die-digital -debatte/sigmar-gabriel-konsequenzen-der-google-debatte-12941865 .html.

POSTFACE

1. https://ec.europa.eu/digital-agenda/en/digital-champions.
2. The Federal Government: *Digital Agenda 2014–2017* (Munich, August 2014), 2, 5. The next quote ibid., 5.

3. Ibid., 27, 31. The next quote ibid., 32.
4. Ibid., 32.
5. Jahresbilanz: Digitale Agenda der Bundesregierung zu einem Viertel umgesetzt; http://www.bitkom.org/Presse/Presseinformation/Jahresbilanz-Digitale-Agenda-der-Bundesregierung-zu-einem-Viertel-umgesetzt.html. Angela Merkel's warning about too much data protection at the congress #CDUdigital on September 12, 2015 in Berlin: https://www.cdu.de/mitgliederkongress.
6. *Digital Agenda 2014–2017*, 12, 5–6. The next quote ibid., 6.
7. Ibid., 16, 14.
8. Ibid., 31.
9. EU data-protection reform: "Council Confirms Agreement with the European Parliament," press release (December 18, 2015), http://www.consilium.europa.eu/en/press/press-releases/2015/12/18-data-protection.
10. Viktor Meyer-Schönberger and Kenneth Cukier, *Big Data: A Revolution That Will Transform How We Live, Work, and Think* (New York: Houghton Mifflin Harcourt, 2013).

INDEX

AADP. *See* Association of Activists of
    Data Protection
adiaphorization, 29, 58
Adorno, Theodor, 28, 45, 56, 84, 113–14,
    117, 120
aesthetic theory, big-data mining influ-
    encing, 62
Airbnb, 122
algorithms, 114, 137n1; consumerism and,
    57–58, 138n8; control and surveillance
    from, 53–54; cultural history represen-
    tation of, 50–51; cybernetics and, 56;
    for digital humanities, 80; Flu Trend
    inaccurate due to, 77–78; historical
    analogy on, 56–57; information man-
    agement from, 53; knowledge from, 55;
    moral human activity freed by, 57; per-
    sonalization of, 52; rationality reduced
    by, 57; responsibility needed for, 58;
    science influenced by, 77; society
    affected by, 51, 56; standardization of,
    58; technocratic rationality of, xv, 56;
    unwanted consequences of, 51–52, 55
algorithmic regulation, xv, 56; for elec-
    tronic card, 27–28; of Internet, 123
Alteration of a Suburban House (Graham),
    18
altruism, 14–15, 131n8
Amazon, 52, 116
American technologies, German culture
    and, 11–12
anonymity, 9
Apple Maps, 90
Arendt, Hannah, 88–89

Association of Activists of Data Protec-
    tion (AADP), 31–32
autological memory, 93

Bacon, Francis, 43, 102
Barlow, Perry, 11
Baum, Gerhart, 21, 119
Bauman, Zygmunt, 14, 28, 29, 97
behavioral patterns, 10–11
Bentham, Jeremy, 97, 102
Berners-Lee, Tim, 82, 116, 117
Big Brother, xv, 100
Big Data (Mayer-Schönberger and
    Cukier), 27, 44, 127
big-data analysts, profile puzzle for, 10
big-data business: mood management
    and, 37–38; society development and,
    126–27
big-data mining, 37; absence of theory
    and, 61–62; aesthetic theory and
    historiography influenced by, 62;
    boycott and, 104; consumerism and,
    48; correlations influenced by, 60,
    62–64; empowerment through, 62;
    encryption and, 104; evasion of, 104;
    fear of, xv; by Google, 99–100; Gross
    National Happiness Index and, 68;
    indifference on, 47–48; as logical
    consequence, xvii; power created by,
    75; problems solved by, 117; sublime
    of, 62–63
books, data affecting, 41, 134n4
boycott, 104
Bunz, Mercedes, 46

business world, data protection in, 19–20

Campbell, Donald T., 78
Campbell's Law, 78–79
Carr, Nicholas, 92
Chamisso, Adelbert von, 69, 70, 102
Circle, The (Eggers), 71
close reading, 85
Close to the Machine: Technophilia and Its Discontents (Ullman), 30
Coca-Cola, surveillance commercial by, 100–101, 146n6
cold civil war, xv, 31
communication: linguistic to visual transition of, 108–9, 148n6; as manipulation, 74; measurement-friendly forms of, 69; by Snapchat, 107–8
communicative capital: commodified, 36; integration of, 35–36
competition: created by Internet, 72–73; created by self-tracking, 73
computational subject, 87
consumer: classification and customization of, 48; data mining and preferences of, 25, 103; Google's knowledge of, 99–100; market-driven customization for, 41; marketing consultants researching preferences of, 20; protection of, 125; rating system affecting behavior of, 122; self-improvement of, 114–15; transparency of, 19–20, 70
consumerism: algorithms and, 57–58, 138n8; big-data mining and, 48; information, 16, 25; Internet and, 115; surveillance and, 47–48
copyright, 123
correlations: big-data mining influencing, 60, 62–64; as objective, 60; strong vs. weak, 60
crowdsourcing, 121, 124
Cukier, Kenneth, 27, 44, 110, 127
cultural analytics, 81
Culture of Control (Garland), 30
cybernetics, 27; algorithms and, 56; data mining and, 32

D'Aloisio, Nick, 40, 89
data, 129n1; acquisition of, 70–71; ambivalent love of, xiii–xiv; analogue life among, 114–15; behavioral patterns decoded by, 10–11; books affected by, 41, 135n4; commercialization of, 18; cultural criticism of, 22, 133n8; discrete, 92; distortion of, 104; efficacy

of, 59–60; erasing of, 23; harmless, 9; ideology dissolved by, 61; Internet accumulating, 17; interpretation of, 68; laws of democracy and, 9, 49; linked, 82; money made from, 68–69; online existences shadowed by, 69; processing of, 81; recombination of, 87; research based on, 60, 139n2; retention of, 8; security of, 8; self-censorship and identity management with, 44–45; selling of, 19; sharing of, 70–71; society of, 77; state efficiency from, 19; theorising from absence of, 61; traces of, 70
data analysis, xvii; price for, 75; therapy, 105
data capitalism, 120
data catastrophe, xiv; environmental catastrophe and, 21–23; ignorance and indifference resulting in, 22–23; prevention of, 20; psychosociological perspective of, 22
data collection: by apps, 117; government and, 126; indifference regarding, 146n6; intelligence agency logic and, 7; lack of responsibility for, 47; measurements and, 68; methodical defects in, 60; population ignorance and, 117, 148n6
datafication, 28, 54
data hack, 103
data love, 92; double-edged potentiality of, xiv; as emotional reaction, 63; as euphemism, xii–xiii; Internet activists embracing, xiii; phenomenon of, xiii; principles of, xiii; privacy and, 37–38; self-tracking and, 13–15
data mining, xiii; adventure of, 37–38; consumer preference and, 25, 103; cybernetic communication and, 32; data intermediaries and, 37; education on, 102; government and, 27; information trading and, 38; profiting from, 38; relationships from, 102–3; responsibility needed for, 58; Snapchat and, 108–9; social reading and, 40–41, 135n3; society's future and, 36; Summly app for, 40. *See also* big-data mining
data protection: in business world, 19–20; cold civil war and, 31; compromised, 100; German government and, 123–25; governments and, 19; international terrorism and, 5; population ignorance of, 9; self-attempt at, 8–9; software developers sensitized by, 25
Declaration of the Independence of Cyberspace (Barlow), 11

Index ✦ 153

Deleuze, Gilles, 27, 32, 45
democracy, 74–76
Dialectic of Enlightenment (Horkheimer and Adorno), 28
Digfit, 13, 73
Digital Agenda, 123–25
Digital Champions, 123
digital Fukushima, 9
digital humanities, 60–61; algorithms for, 80; culture of reasoning and, 84; distant and close reading for, 85; hypertext and, 85–86; nanopublication and, 83; quantity vs. quality in, 81–82; subjectiveness of, 81; telling to tallying text influencing, 85
digital media, 98; binary operational mode of, 69; education needed for, 121; growth of, 125–26; information control and, 53; in primary schools, 123–24
digital orientalism, 45
digital revolution, German government and, 124
digitization, 28, 54, 60–61
discrete data, 92
distant reading, 7, 81, 85
Dürrenmatt, Friedrich, 55, 102

Eggers, Dave, 71
electronic card, algorithmic regulation for, 27–28
employee tracking, 30, 73, 134n8, 141n3
encryption, 11, 104
Enlightenment, xiii, xvii, 41, 88; dark side of, xv; transparency and, 111
environmental catastrophe, 21–23
epistemological revolution, 60, 82
EU Data Protection Reform, 126–27

Facebook, 27, 35, 52, 72, 76, 116; big-data mining by, 101; information archiving of, 106
Farecast, 38, 39
filter bubble, 52–53
Filter Bubble, The: How the New Personalized Web Is Changing What We Read and How We Think (Pariser), 52
Fitbit, 13, 73
Flu Trend (Google), 77–78
Frankfurter Allgemeine Zeitung, 21, 119
Free Rainer—Dein Fernseher Lügt (Weingartner), 103–4
Fukuyama, Francis, 48, 114

gamification, 72

Garland, David, 30
Garvey, Angelo, 46
German culture, American technologies and, 11–12
German Democratic Republic, 5–6, 7
German Federal Intelligence Service, NSA scandal and, 5
German government: data protection and, 123–25; digital revolution and, 124; technology neutrality of, 125
German Ministry of the Internet (MOTI), 31
Gitelman, Lisa, 60
God's eye, 98–99
Google, 27; big-data mining by, 99–100; categorization improvements by, 16; consumer knowledge from, 99–100; efficacy of, 99; power misuse by, 120; search results from, 52; security of, 115–16; self-presentation of, 99; Snapchat and, 106
Google Chrome, 104
Google Drive, 57
Google Glass, 16, 17–18, 54, 99, 106
Google Maps, 90
government: data collection and, 126; data mining and, 27; data protection and, 19; new ministry of the Internet proposed by, 121; NSA scandal and, 8, 12; on power of Internet, 120
GPS tracking, 32, 135n5
Graham, Dan, 18
Gross National Happiness Index (Facebook), 68
Guardian, 3, 24, 115

Hapifork, 39, 46, 73
Hapilabs, 39
Hedonometer.org, 68, 77, 78, 142n9
Heller, Christian, 5–6
historiography, big-data mining influencing, 62
Horkheimer, Max, 28
How Algorithms Are Changing Knowledge, Work, Public Life, and Politics Without Making a Lot of Noise (Bunz), 46
human behavior, absence of theory and, 59
Human-Computer Interaction Lab, 105
Human Face of Big Data, The, 44
human liberation, 15–16
Humboldtian educational ideal, 87
hyperreading, 41, 92
hypertext, 85–86, 92

Hypertext: The Convergence of Contemporary Critical Theory and Technology (Landow), 86

if-then directives, xv, 50, 59
I Like What I See (app), 104
Imperative of Responsibility, The: In Search of an Ethics for the Technological Age (Jonas), 21
individual freedom, collective knowledge and, 55
influence index, in social network, 36
information, 129n1; algorithms for management of, 53; consumerism, 16, 25; data mining and trading, 38; digital media for control of, 53; Facebook's archiving of, 106; filters needed for, 111; at fingertips, xii; freedom of, 118; liberation from, 90; love for, xi; overload of, 40; self-tracking for, 14
Instagram, 72
instrumental rationality, 28
intelligence agency: data collection and, 7; data erasing and, 23; effectiveness of, 6; Internet collaboration by, 18–19; logic of, 3–7; market consultants compared to, 19–20; security and, 6–7; snooping of, 25
intelligent trash container, 18
international terrorism, data protection and, 5
Internet: algorithmic regulation of, 123; competition created from, 72–73; consumerism predominating, 115; data accumulation from, 17; disillusion of, 118; filter bubble used with, 52–53; freedom of, 26–27; government on power of, 120; intelligence agencies collaborating with, 18–19; as lifestyle disease, 11; memory of, 47, 105, 109; monitoring of, 97–98; national laws attempting to bind, 8; as neocolonialism, 11; networking and, 26; neutrality, 25–26; ownership of, 24–25; policy needed for, 119–20; self-censorship and identity management with, 44–45; silent revolution driven by, 44; society influenced by, 116; two-class problem of, 26; utopian and heterotopian promise of, 42, 118, 136n6

Jawbone's Wristband, 13
Jonas, Hans, 21, 29, 118

Kindle, 40
KLM (Dutch airline), 100
Klout score, 35–36, 42, 46
knowledge, 129n1, 145n12; acquisition of, 87; from algorithms, 55; democratization of, 82; dissection of, 92; of Google's consumers, 99–100; hyperreading changing approach to, 92; increase and undermining of, 76; individual freedom and collective, 55; juggling of, 87–88, 93; Lessing on, 89; nanopublication and, 83; as numerical, 77; process-oriented to result-oriented approach to, 89; stabilization of, 90–91; Weinberger on, 91–92
Kubrick, Stanley, 46

Landow, George P., 86
laws of democracy, data and, 9, 49
Lessing, Gotthold Ephraim, 88–89, 102
linked data, 82
Liquid Surveillance: A Conversation (Bauman), 29
Lyotard, Jean-François, 62–64

market-driven customization, 41
marketing consultants: customer preference researched by, 20; intelligence agencies compared to, 19–20
Mayer-Schönberger, Viktor, 27, 44, 110, 127
McLuhan, Marshall, 15, 30
measurement: advanced methods of, 105; communication forms and, 69; data collection and, 68; quantification from, 70; rationality and, 67
Meckel, Miriam, 46
media: agenda of, xvii; as extensions of man, 15–16; literacy of, 102, 147n1; social realm determining, 48. *See also* digital media
Microsoft, 38
Mill, John Stuart, 54
Modernity and the Holocaust (Bauman), 28
mood management, big-data business and, 37–38
moral human activity, 57
moral mercilessness, 28–29
moral responsibility, technological developments outsourcing of, 29
Morozov, Evgeny, 13, 15, 18–19, 45, 115, 119; information consumerism and, 25; legislation demanded by, 20; on surveillance, 21
MOTI. *See* German Ministry of the Internet

nanopub.com, 83
nanopublication, 82, 143n4; digital
    humanities and, 83; knowledge and, 83;
    of navigation, 90
Nathan the Wise (Lessing), 89
National Security Agency of the United
    States (NSA) scandal, xiv; citizen
    movement from, 6; country's reaction
    to, 4; German Federal Intelligence
    Service and, 5; government and political
    helplessness during, 8, 12; international
    dimensions of, 11–12; intranational
    tension from, 11–12; lack of protest in, 31;
    Obama and, 4–5; population ignorance
    and, 9; surveillance practices and, 3
Negative Dialectics (Adorno), 84
neocolonialism, Internet as, 11
Netflix, 41, 52
networking computers, 26, 51
netzpolitik.org, 26
*Next. Erinnerungen an eine Zukunft ohne
    uns* (Meckel), 46
Nova Atlantis (Bacon), 43, 102
NSA. *See* National Security Agency of the
    United States scandal
numeratocracy, 70
numerical-mathematical rationality, 74
Nymi wristband, 27

Obama, Barack, 4–5
On Liberty (Mill), 54
online existences, data shadowing, 69
ontologies, 83, 144n8

panopticon, 97
Panopticon (Bentham), 102
Pariser, Eli, 52
personal data: exploitation of, xiv–xv;
    extrospective and introspective variety
    of, 20
Peter Schlemihl (Chamisso), 69, 70, 102
Philosophical and Theological Writings
    (Lessing), 88
Physicians, The (Dürrenmatt), 55, 102
population ignorance: appeasement of, 9;
    regarding data collection, 117, 148n6;
    regarding data protection and surveil-
    lance, 9
postmodern theory, hypertext and, 86
Post-Privacy (Heller), 5–6
"Postscript on the Societies of Control"
    (Deleuze), 27
privacy: context of, xvi–xvii; data love and,
    37–38; data mining and, xiii; education

on, 110; future of, 115; Google and, xvi;
    as inalienable right, xv; protection of,
    21; Snapchat and, 107; surveillance
    and, 5
privacy breach: sensitivity of, 10–11; smart
    things and, 16. *See also* data hack

rationality, 57, 67; instrumental, 28; numeri-
    cal-mathematical, 74; technocratic,
    xv, 56
"Raw Data" Is an Oxymoron (Gitelman),
    60
RDF. *See* Resource Description
    Framework
Rejoinder, A (Lessing), 88, 102
Resource Description Framework (RDF),
    82

Schirrmacher, Frank, 21, 119
Schmidt, Eric, 44, 99, 106, 115
science: algorithmic data influencing,
    77; society's relationship with, 15;
    statistical evaluation for, 78–79
Secret Intelligence Service, 23
security: of data, 8; of Google, 115–16;
    intelligence agency logic and, 6–7; as
    superfundamental right, 6
self-reification, 28
self-tracking, 82; altruistic aspect of, 14–15,
    131n8; competition among, 73; culture
    of, 13–14; data love and, 13–15; informa-
    tion available for, 14; as intelligent
    trash container, 18; obsession of, 15; sci-
    ence and society relationship changed
    by, 15; self-awareness of, 14
semantic web, 82, 83, 86, 91, 143n6
*Shallows, The: How the Internet Is Changing
    the Way We Think, Read, and Remember*
    (Carr), 92
silent revolution: doom from, 47; explo-
    siveness of, 46; halting of, 48–49;
    Internet driving, 44
Silent Revolution, The (Bunz), 46
*Silent Revolution, The: Or, the Future Effects
    of Steam and Electricity Upon the Con-
    dition of Mankind* (Garvey), 46
Singer, Peter, 5
smart things: atrophy caused by, 16; human
    liberation provided by, 15; privacy
    breach and, 16
Snapchat, 105; communication by, 107–8;
    data mining and, 108–9; financial
    strength of, 106–7; Google and, 106;
    privacy and, 107

Snowden, Edward, 3, 23, 115, 117, 119; hero-
    ism of, 24–25; Obama on, 4–5; support
    for, 4
social engineer: age and values of, 42;
    problem solving of, 39; software
    programmers as, 42–43; standardiza-
    tion of, 57–58
social markups, 83
social network, influence index in, 36
social reading, 40–41, 135n3
social science, computational, 54–55
society: algorithms affecting, 51, 56; big-
    data business developed of, 126–27;
    contradictory nature of, 30; of data, 77;
    data mining and future of, 36; digitiza-
    tion of, 28; improvement of, 114–15;
    Internet influencing, 116; misdoings
    treated by, 111; ranking differentiations
    created by, 35–36; science relationship
    with, 15; technology and, 115
sociometer, 54
software developers, 25, 42–43
Spotify (app), 123
statistics, 72; analytical criteria influenc-
    ing, 78; attractiveness of, 70; control
    increased by, 75; culture fostered by,
    76; democracy and, 74–75; distortion
    among, 77–78; identity created by,
    73; scientific quality evaluation from,
    78–79
Stiegler, Bernard, 92
stock-market algorithms, 46, 68–69, 141n3
sublime: absence of theory influencing,
    63; of big-data mining, 62–63; disaster
    of, 63
Summly (app), 40, 42, 46
surveillance: algorithms for, 53–54; Coca-
    Cola's commercial regarding, 100–101,
    146n6; consumerism and, 47–48; dis-
    course of, 97–98; lack of responsibility
    regarding, 47; Morozov on, 21; NSA
    scandal from practices of, 3; population
    ignorance regarding, 9; privacy and, 5;
    problem of, 16; research, 98; technol-
    ogy influencing, 7
synopticon, 98

Taking Care of Youth and the Generations
    (Stiegler), 92
technocratic rationality, xv, 56

technological determinism, 48
technology: corruption and irregularities
    policed from, 45; denial for, 104–5; dis-
    contentment for development of, 112;
    education on, 102, 110; efficiency from,
    29–30; employee tracking and, 30, 73,
    134n8, 141n3; ever present, 113; Ger-
    man culture and, 11–12; of hypertext,
    86; neutrality of, 45, 125; possibilities
    offered by, 29–30; power produced by,
    45; society and, 115; success of, 29, 42;
    surveillance influenced by, 7
theory, absence of: big-data mining and,
    61–62; correlations with, 60; human
    behavior and, 59; humanities digitized
    and, 60–61; sublime influenced by,
    63
theory fatigue, 63
theyrule.net, 111
transparency, xiv; absoluteness of, 13–14;
    advocacy for, 9; of consumers, 19–20,
    70; culture of, 121; democracy and, 76;
    Enlightenment and, 111; intelligence
    agency logic and, 7; social implemen-
    tation of, 23; social reading and, 41
tripel, 83, 143n5
Truman Show, The (Weir), 18
truth, disputes from, 88–89
Twitter, 53, 72, 101
2001: A Space Odyssey (Kubrick), 46

Uber, 122–23
Ullman, Ellen, 30

"Visible Man, The: Ethics in a World
    Without Secrets" (Singer), 5

Weblogs, 101
Weinberger, David, 91–92
Weingartner, Hans, 103–4
Weir, Peter, 18
Whistle.im, 10–11
WikiLeaks, 4, 111
Wikipedia, 27, 90, 121
World Wide Web, 82, 116

Yahoo, 40
YouTube, 115

Zuckerberg, Mark, 45, 106